HORIZON

SPRING, 1970 · VOLUME XII, NUMBER 2

Back to School

In his book *The Making of a Counter Culture* Theodore Roszak quotes a course description from an "anti-university." Called "From Comic Books to the Dance of Shiva: Spiritual Amnesia and the Physiology of Self-Estrangement," the course consists of "A free-wheeling succession of open-ended situations. Ongoing vibrations highly relevant. Exploration of Inner Space, de-conditioning of human robot, significance of psycho-chemicals, and the transformation of Western European Man. Source material: Artaud, Zimmer, Gurdjieff, W. Reich, K. Marx, Gnostic, Sufi, and Tantric texts, autobiographical accounts of madness and ecstatic states of consciousness—Pop art and twentieth century prose."

Somehow, school doesn't sound the same any more. Whatever happened to Plato, to Descartes, to Voltaire and Jane Austen? Where is the old Western Civ course, from the Glory that was Greece to the End of Imperialism? And the survey of science from Archimedes to Copernicus and Francis Bacon? What, after all, has happened to the rationalist, Enlightenment tradition? Are these kids mad?

Yes. Or, if not mad, they are at least uncomfortable with the traditions they have inherited, and they are feverishly exploring all those men and ideas that their elders ignored or passed over lightly in their educations: the mystics, the madmen, the antirationalists and the seers, demonology and shamanism, astrology and witchcraft. They are in flight from reason, as the Enlightenment understood reason; they are intent upon finding, or making, a new tradition.

Bosch group, circa 1500

Snyder group, Stockbridge, 1970

HORIZON
A Magazine of the Arts

SPRING, 1970 · VOLUME XII, NUMBER 2

An upheaval of this sort is often simple enough to discern. To define it, to know where it will lead, is impossible. Yet it seems a fundamental enough aberration, or lasting change, in the course of civilization to merit extended attention. In this issue, therefore, we present some of the signs of the flight from reason (see Thomas Meehan's article and Don Snyder's pictures beginning on page 4), some of the heroes of the counter culture (Herman Hesse, page 28, and Antonin Artaud, page 48), and an intriguing historical precedent (the anchorites, page 22). Peter Gay has written an essay on the Enlightenment and what it still has to say to us (page 40), and Lawrence Malkin has written about George Orwell's novel *1984*—the totalitarian *reductio ad absurdum* of liberal rationalism. In an article on Hieronymus Bosch that begins on page 66 Gilbert Highet finds a striking contemporaneity in Bosch's great masterpiece *The Garden of Earthly Delights*. Beginning on page 56 there appears an essay on the Daedalus myth by our old friend Michael Ayrton, who thinks he might be that ancient Athenian—just to show that the kids have no monopoly on The Movement. And on page 82 Alvin Toffler offers an explanation of why the flight from reason should occur just now.

If our table of contents reads a trifle like the course description at an anti-university, well, we can only say we are not trying to invent new systems; our attempt is to present an open-ended, consciousness-expanding set of ongoing vibrations. Or something like that.   —C.L.M.

HORIZON is published every three months by American Heritage Publishing Co., Inc. Editorial and executive offices: 551 Fifth Avenue, New York, N.Y. 10017. Treasurer: George W. Breitkreuz. Secretary: John C. Taylor 3rd. All correspondence about subscriptions should be addressed to: HORIZON Subscription Office, 379 West Center St., Marion, Ohio 43302.

Single Copies: $6.00. Subscriptions: $20.00 per year in the U.S. & Canada; elsewhere, $21.00

Cumulative indexes for Volumes I–V and VI–X are available at $3. HORIZON is also indexed in the *Readers' Guide to Periodical Literature.* The editors welcome contributions but can assume no responsibility for unsolicited material. Title registered U.S. Patent Office. Second class postage paid at New York, N.Y., and at additional mailing offices.

COVER: Life in the central panel of Hieronymus Bosch's greatest painting, often called *The Garden of Earthly Delights,* is unencumbered by conscience, clothing, or cognizance of any higher goal than pleasure. There has been no more enigmatic painter than Bosch, with his air-borne fishes, ubiquitous birds, and such curiously ingenuous hedonists as the couple in this detail. The painting, a triptych measuring 7′ 2″ × 12′ 9″, has fascinated generations of visitors to Madrid's Museo del Prado, but what its message may be is a question that has long been debated by authorities. Gilbert Highet puts forth an original and provocative interpretation in an article that begins on page 66. The photograph is from Holle Verlag.

ON THIS SITE IN FEDERAL HALL
APRIL 30 1789
GEORGE WASHINGTON
TOOK THE OATH AS THE FIRST PRESIDENT
OF THE UNITED STATES
OF AMERICA

THE FLIGHT FROM REASON

"It is one of the major paradoxes of our time that the best educated and the most sophisticated generation of young Americans in history should seriously believe not only in astrology but also in areas of the occult like palmistry, numerology, tarot cards, and witchcraft, formerly a twilight zone occupied by crackpot old ladies." Great Buddha, could they be right?

On the steps of the old subtreasury building near Wall Street (opposite) George Washington gives his benediction to swaying, chanting members of the International Society for Krishna Consciousness. There are twenty-one Krishna temples in America, some of them communes in which men and women live together. The youngsters in this photograph, all of them Americans, are for the most part New Yorkers. The girls live in their own apartments, the boys live at a temple on lower Second Avenue. Both sexes gather at the temple for meals, meditation sessions, and other rituals. Krishna Consciousness, according to its spiritual leader His Divine Grace A. C. Bhaktivedanta Swami, "is the Science of God realization." In the present age, "called the Age of Kali (hypocrisy and quarrel) the method of liberation prescribed by the Scriptures is to chant the Holy Names of God continually." The mantra is chanted while swaying (hand clapping optional): "Hare Krishna, Hare Krishna, Krishna Krishna, Hare Hare/ Hare Rama, Hare Rama, Rama Rama, Hare Hare."

Of course, everyone is, and always has been, slightly mad. Still, repressing the unreasonable side of his nature, man in the Western world has, since the eighteenth century, built a civilization based on scientific reason and classic Aristotelian logic—the heritage of the Enlightenment. And the result, especially in this country during the past fifty years, has been a rational society that has made one technological breakthrough after another, from the invention of the pop-up toaster to the ability to land men on the moon. Here, until recently, two plus two had inevitably equaled four, not five, as Eastern mystics suggest, and no one other than J. D. Salinger had been able to imagine the sound of one hand clapping.

In the past three or four years, however, embracing everything from A to Zen, a significant number of Americans have entered upon a headlong flight from reason, a mass retreat into mysticism, superstition, occultism, the unreality of drugs, irrationality, antirationality, and pararationality in a myriad of forms, up to and including the installation in one of the White House offices of an "executive sandbox" in which Presidential aides could relax by reverting to mindless childhood play. In the delicate human balance between sanity and madness, madness seems to be gaining the upper hand.

This writer, who has always considered himself virtually an eighteenth-century philosophe, scorning illogic and unreason, had been unaware of the proportions of the flight from reason until last summer. Since then, however, although not a sociologist, a psychologist, or a historian, but merely a thirty-eight-year-old observer with a liberal arts degree in English and an edgy interest in American goings on, I have done a good deal of looking into the matter. As a result I may yet end up with a deck of tarot cards in hand.

By THOMAS MEEHAN

The occasion that drew my attention to the flight from reason was the so-called Woodstock Music and Art Fair. In Bethel, New York, on the weekend of August 15, 1969, only twenty-seven days after Neil Armstrong first stepped on the moon, some four hundred thousand under-thirty Americans sat hunched in the rain on a drenched and muddy hillside listening passively hour after hour to a concert of rock and folk music. For the most part they were under the influence of drugs—marijuana, hashish, amphetamines, and LSD. This happening, or concert, which attracted the largest live audience of any kind in the history of the world, has been called the dawning of the Age of Aquarius, a time when love, peace, and tranquillity will dominate the earth. Perhaps. More significantly, I'd suggest, it marked the dramatic rise to the surface of an Age of Unreason that by August 16, 1969, had not only dawned but had already reached somewhere around eight o'clock in the morning. The striking revelation of the Woodstock Music and Art Fair was that the United States had almost an entire generation—and not simply a relative handful, as had earlier been assumed—of Dionysian anarchists who had abandoned reason.

Of course, the young have always been anarchic and rebellious, but this generation, most observers agree, is unique in rejecting not only the superficial life-style of its elders but rational thought itself. Thousands of young people, in fact—and the number is increasing each month—have dropped entirely out of society, many to live instead in rural communes where they alternately spend their anti-intellectual days as frontier pioneers, chopping wood, drawing water from streams, building rude shacks, and farming, or as Tennysonian lotus-eaters, stringing beads and chanting Eastern mantras. It is unrealistic, say the sociologists, to assume that America's disaffected young are merely going through a phase and that the marijuana-smoking hippie with hair to his shoulders will

soon be toting a Mark Cross attaché case to his job at IBM. No, many thousands have chosen unreason as a permanent way of life. Admittedly, the flight from reason is for the most part a phenomenon of the young, of those under the age of thirty, but it should be remembered that more than 50 per cent of this nation's population is under thirty. Moreover, the young claim that their elders are equally as irrational as they are. To their minds, the exhausted Fairfield County commuter who downs three martinis after his return home to Cos Cob from his job in New York, and who then spends his evening glazedly watching television reruns of "Perry Mason" and "Run For Your Life," is behaving every bit as unreasonably as the marijuana smoker staring at a psychedelic light box in an East Village pad. Perhaps so, though as a martini-drinker and Perry Mason aficionado myself, I'm inclined to disagree with the young on this point. On the other hand, I'm willing to concede that the madman never realizes himself to be mad. In short, it's possible that we're all far crazier than we know.

Nowhere is the flight from reason more evident than in the world of contemporary art, and indeed, if art genuinely reflects life, then madness is already upon all of us to a greater degree than anyone has dreamed. A few years ago, when pop art raised its head, everyone assumed that art had gone far-out enough. In contrast with some of the things that are now being created and appear in exhibitions as art, however, works of pop art like the Campbell's soup can by Andy Warhol virtually rival the ceiling of the Sistine Chapel. Consider, for instance, Impossible Art. According to *Art in America*, one of the sanest art magazines in the United States, Impossible Art is causing "a violent upheaval in the art worlds of America and Europe, and attacking the art establishments of dealers, private collectors, galleries, mu-

seums, critics, and art historians in much the same way that students are attacking college institutions." And what is Impossible Art? It is such an aesthetic endeavor as this: digging a grave in New York's Central Park and then filling it up again, as Claes Oldenburg did a while ago. "I was able to create from earth an invisible sculpture of negative and positive spaces," commented Oldenburg.

Impossible Art takes a number of forms, among them Earthworks, Site Sculpture, Skyworks, and Nihilworks. Oldenburg's grave is, or was, an Earthwork, as is "Circumflex," a work by an artist named Mike Heizer that is nothing more than a 120-foot-long ditch that Heizer dug one day at Massacre Dry Lake in Nevada. "Duration Piece #9," a work of Site Sculpture by Douglas Huebler, a forty-five-year-old New York artist, is perhaps best described in his own words:

"On January 9, 1969 a clear plastic box measuring 1″ x 1″ x ¾″ was enclosed within a slightly larger cardboard container that was sent by registered mail to an address in Berkeley, California. Upon being returned as 'undeliverable' it was left altogether intact and enclosed within another slightly larger container and sent again as registered mail to Riverton, Utah—and once more returned to the sender as undeliverable. Similarly another container enclosing all previous containers was sent to Ellsworth, Nebraska; similarly to Alpha, Iowa; similarly to Tuscola, Michigan; similarly and finally to Hull, Massachusetts which accomplished the 'marking' of a line joining the two coasts of the United States during a period of six weeks of time."

The final container, plus a sheaf of registered-mail receipts, a map, and the above statement, constituted the finished work of Site Sculpture, of which the United States Post Office was an unconscious co-creator. "I like the idea that even as I eat, sleep, or play the work is moving toward its completion," writes Huebler of his Site Sculpture.

The point of Skyworks, say the artists who create them, is "to activate space." For instance, artist Forrest Myers began his Skyworks career by shining beams from four arc-lamps into a night sky and thus, in his own words, creating "a lot of activated space." Nihilworks, as the name suggests, are destructive, and Nihilartists prove their point, whatever that may be, by slashing canvases with knives or setting fire to them, or by creating light sculptures designed to blind the eyes of the viewer. As his contribution, Nihilartist Ralph Ortiz kills chickens. "It is better to kill chickens," Ortiz says, "than to give expression to my killer instincts, which we all have, and murder a person."

Impossible Art is so named, by the way, because in most cases there is virtually no way that it can be seen as an object in a museum, a gallery, or for that matter, anywhere else, unless one is willing, say, to journey to Massacre Dry Lake to gaze at Heizer's ditch. On the other hand, a show of Impossible Art entitled "Live in Your Head— When Attitudes Become Form" was improbably put together in Europe by the Philip Morris corporation and has been shown in Bern, Amsterdam, Krefeld, and London. "Live in Your Head" consists in good part of photographs of works like Heizer's ditch or Dennis Oppenheim's "Cyclonic Extension," a snow-covered field in which a pair of dirt paths were cleared by a snow shovel. The show also includes a Concept Tableau by Edward Kienholz and Jean Tinguely that is made up of a bronze plaque with the words "The American Trip" on it and a typed statement by Kienholz that reads, in part, as follows:

"Starting from Los Angeles, Jean and I will drive by car until we are both compelled by a thing, a place, a situation, etc., to do something. I don't know what it will be, where it will be, what it will cost, whether it will be animal vegetable or mineral, or even bigger than a bread box. It might be alive or explosive."

"Price: Part One $10,000.00 Tinguely
$10,000.00 Kienholz
Part Two $ 1,000.00
Part Three Cost plus artists' wages doubled"

Another form taken by Impossible Art is so-called Street Works, which were first done in New York in the early spring of 1969. In a ten-block area of midtown Manhattan twenty artists one afternoon created the world's first Street Works. Characterized by their creators as "soft, gentle, and practically invisible," Street Works are difficult to describe, but perhaps two examples will suggest what they're all about.

Example 1: John Perreault, an artist-poet and art critic for *The Village Voice*, created a Street Work that he entitled "Street Music." Starting at East 42nd Street and Madison Avenue, he wandered on foot north to West 52nd Street and Sixth Avenue, stopping on his way to make a phone call at every sidewalk booth he came upon. On each occasion he let the phone ring three times and then hung up—thus, "Street Music," "invisible and for the most part inaudible," as Perreault noted later in *The Village Voice*. "Also," added Perreault, "it cost no money since every time I hung up I got my dime back."

Example 2: Bernadette Mayer, a New York artist, contributed something she called "Polaroid Street Work." That is, walking in more or less the same area in which Perreault was making his phone calls, she took a Polaroid picture of the street every block or so, strolled onward for the minute that the picture took to develop, and then attached the finished picture to the nearest surface at hand, usually a fire hydrant or trash basket.

"Totally exhausted," reported Perreault later about his mental state upon completing "Street Music," "I walked over to Sam Goody's, bought an album of sound effects and then went to 42nd Street to see Steve McQueen in *Bullitt*." He did not say how Miss Mayer had survived her afternoon of creative effort.

I was born in the middle of August, which, according to astrologers, makes me a Leo, "proud, magnanimous, self-aware, egotistical, and violent," zodiacal traits I share with Mae West and the late Herbert Hoover. Now, as a rationalist I don't for a moment believe in astrology, but an increasing number of Americans do, and for that reason I've been looking warily into the subject of late. There are, I've discovered, no fewer than 10,000 full-time astrologers practicing today in the United States, plus 175,000 part-time astrologers, both numbers that have tripled in the past five years. Moreover, there are now astrology cookbooks, an astrology marriage-manual, and astrological dating services. Some 1,200 of the nation's 1,750 daily newspapers now run horoscope columns, whereas a few years ago only slightly more than 90 papers carried such columns. And, in a classic combination of logic and illogic, an organization calling itself the Time Pattern Research Institute has fed twenty-five million pieces of astrological information into an IBM 360 computer and programmed it to print out horoscopes. When the time, date, and place of birth of a T.P.R.I. client is put into the computer, a fifteen-thousand-word horoscope emerges in less than two minutes, and at twenty dollars per horoscope, T.P.R.I. reports doing more than ten thousand each month.

In the past even those who secretly believed in astrology were unwilling to admit it publicly, but now all sorts of people, from the Beatles to Marlene Dietrich, speak openly of their faith in astrology. Astrology has not only won millions of converts but has also become respectable. Indeed, not long ago Miss Dietrich tried to get an appointment with U Thant at the United Nations to warn him that the date selected for a special session of the General Assembly was astrologically unsound. Five years ago, one suspects, she wouldn't have dreamed of doing such a thing. And Marshall McLuhan has stated that astrology is "tomorrow's science dreamed today," and "one of the media of the Electric Age." "I *know* I'm a Moon Child, born under the sign of Cancer," says McLuhan, "I can feel it in my veins." Perhaps less surprising, the entire fashion industry is unabashedly hooked on astrology. "The thought of bringing out a collection, or even basting a seam, under unfavorable planetary auspices is enough to reduce designers in New York and Paris to well-publicized hysteria," noted *The New York Times* recently.

But, predictably, it's the nation's young who make up the mass of new believers in astrology. In fact, it is one of the major paradoxes of our time that the best educated and most sophisticated generation of young Americans in history should seriously believe not only in astrology but also in areas of the occult like palmistry, numerology, tarot cards, and witchcraft, formerly a twilight zone occupied by crackpot old ladies. A good many young people today also believe quite literally in the future possibility of things like thought transference—not simply ESP, which they consider old hat, but the ability of people thousands of miles apart to converse by transference of thought, which would eliminate any necessity for the American Telephone & Telegraph Company, thank God. And they believe in mind travel. In the years ahead, they say, thought waves will end the need for spaceships—the mind will by itself travel to the farthest reaches of the universe. A few years ago such ideas would rarely have been heard outside the confines of a padded cell, but now, in the Age of Unreason, they are becoming increasingly common and as matter-of-factly accepted as the theorems of Euclidean geometry.

If one were asked to select an area of American life in which the flight from reason hadn't yet become evident, the choice might well be Big Business, the hardheaded world of corporations like General Electric, Humble Oil, and Southern California Edison. Yet, scores of companies such as these have for the past several years been involving themselves in a form of psychology called sensitivity training, a program in which groups of ten to forty people, called encounter groups, are locked in together for anywhere from a weekend to two weeks, and under the direction of a so-called trainer, are urged to touch one another, to embrace, and to speak out at length upon whatever happens to be on their minds. They are instructed to say exactly what they think of one another, no matter how insulting an opinion may be ("You put me off because you have a weight problem," says one woman to another in a typical instance), to discuss openly their innermost feelings about their jobs, their families, and of course their sex lives, and in general to voice any angers, hatreds, anxieties, or frustrations they may be harboring. At the Esalen Institute at Big Sur, California, the nation's leading center for sensitivity training, encounter groups of mixed gentlemen and ladies sometimes meet in the nude, sitting hip-deep in a shallow swimming pool, though most other centers that run sensitivity-training programs suggest that the participants try to keep at least a few clothes on, if only a wrapped-around towel or sheet.

The theory behind sensitivity training—scorned by psychologists and psychiatrists of more traditional disciplines, who equate it, at best, with crash dieting at a fat farm—is that the brute who enters the progam with all the sensitivity of a defense lineman for the Baltimore Colts will emerge with the quivering nerves of a lyric poet. And large corporations and educational establishments all over the country are shipping their employees off to sensitivity-training programs, paying as much as a hundred dollars a day per employee, to the point where sensitivity training has itself become Big Business.

Corporation executives who contend that sensitivity training is valuable say that it helps workers to have a greater understanding of one another's problems and points of view. Almost everyone agrees that sensitivity training does *something* to those who undergo it, but perhaps not always what is intended. A division manager of a large corporation was described before being put through training as "a ferocious guy—brilliant, but a thoroughgoing autocrat—who everyone agreed was just what the division needed because it was in a tough, competitive business." In sensitivity training, however, going through the program with a dozen of his underlings, the division manager found out exactly what everyone thought of him, and "his effectiveness fell apart. . . . The reason he'd been so good was that he didn't realize what a beast he was." The training can backfire in other ways, too. Some have had nervous breakdowns during sensitivity training, and have become so acutely sensitive that they have quit their corporate jobs. One sensitized California advertising executive, for instance, left a job paying nearly $100,000 per year to become a dishwasher at the Esalen Institute, which is perhaps one way for such a place to recruit scarce kitchen help. Of course not everyone responds as favorably to sensitivity trainers as Esalen's new dishwasher; for the last word from the rationalist camp, see the letter my friend Jean Stafford wrote to the director of one such program [page 120].

One could go on and on citing examples of present-day madness and the flight from reason—off-Broadway nonplays in which the evening consists mainly of nudes grunting and groping about; musical compositions scored for automobile engines and jackhammers; a New York nightclub where the customers sit naked, if they choose, under sheets while listening to tranquilizing music and playing with toys such as balloons and kaleidoscopes; be-in's; fat-in's; happenings. But, in a society that has always before been essentially rational, the question that most perplexes me is *why* are so many turning away from reason? Admittedly, some of the behavior that we interpret here as madness or unreason, like a belief in Zen, is considered perfectly sane and reasonable in vast portions of the world, as in most of Asia, for instance. Nonetheless, in the context of American society, to believe in Eastern mysticism or astrology or palmistry must be considered at least unusual. Again, *why* are so many joining the flight from reason? Psychologists, sociologists, and historians, I've discovered, offer several possible answers.

First, there are observers who see a marked historical parallel between patterns of behavior in the United States during the past twenty-five years, since Hiroshima, and the behavior of Europeans during the fifteenth and sixteenth centuries. In the latter half of the fifteenth century, as the French writer and psychologist Michel Foucault notes in his book *Madness and Civilization*, Europe, afflicted by the plague, was obsessed by death and the fear of death.* As the sixteenth century began, however, the obsession with death was replaced by an obsession with madness and a celebration of insanity in which the madman was applauded as a hero. This is the period in which Hieronymus Bosch painted *The Ship of Fools, The Garden of Earthly Delights*, and *The Temptation of Saint Anthony*. In the latter painting Bosch depicts madness as itself a temptation to rational and moral man, suggesting that the inner world of fantasy, of dreams, and of insane hallucinations, however frightening, was more attractive to sixteenth-century man than the ugly reality of a life that necessarily ended in death. In short, the retreat into madness was nothing more than a way to repress the thought of death—"the lunatic, anticipating the macabre, has disarmed it."

Those who see a parallel between those times and our own point out that from Hiroshima until about the time of the assassination of President Kennedy, the United States, as well as much of the rest of the world, was obsessed by the fear of death by nuclear attack. This is the time of Beckett's *End-*

*An article on Foucault appears in the Autumn, 1969, issue of HORIZON.

game, of films like *On the Beach* and *Dr. Strangelove*, of bomb-shelter building, of John Foster Dulles and brinkmanship, and of widespread American paranoia about the threat of Russian attack. Of course, this fear still persists among some, or else the United States wouldn't be building the Safeguard ABM system. To a large degree, however, Americans, and especially young Americans, have repressed the fear of nuclear death and have turned instead to an obsession with madness, just as the sixteenth-century Europeans did. Films like *Morgan!* are our equivalent of Bosch's *Garden of Earthly Delights*.

Paradoxically, those young Americans who have chosen illogic as a way of life have used the classic process of reasoning to arrive at a rationale for their unreason. If reason has led man to create nuclear weapons and to fight wars that have since 1914 killed some one hundred million persons, they argue, then reason itself is suspect, leaving only the alternative of unreason. In short, as the young see it, if Hitler and Stalin were sane, they'd prefer not to be: if Dr. Edward Teller, Herman Kahn, and Secretary of Defense Laird are reasonable, they'll take astrology. Besides, they add, if everyone is so close to death, if the bombs are certain to fall eventually, then life itself is purposeless, and what reason is there in reason? And, substituting the plague for the bomb, this is exactly how the sixteenth-century Europeans felt.

Other thinkers, like Herbert Marcuse, however, argue that the flight from reason is caused by circumstances that didn't obtain in the sixteenth century, that is, the pressures placed upon all of us by a supertechnological and rapidly changing society. In a book entitled *Future Shock*, an excerpt of which appears farther on in this magazine, Alvin Toffler suggests that those who have joined the flight from reason are suffering from a previously unknown form of physical and mental ill-

ness that, as the title of his book indicates, he has chosen to call future shock. Future shock, says Toffler, is brought on by incessant, rapid change and by the ceaseless bombardment of everyone's senses with television, radio, newspapers, magazines, books, movies, traffic noises, pneumatic drills, etc., etc.; a never-ending mixed-media show in which one is inescapably trapped, assaulted by everything from Anacin commercials to *The New York Times, Life* magazine, and roadside neon signs flashing the words "Jesus Saves." There are, says Toffler, a great number of people in the United States who simply can't stand up to this pressure. The victim of future shock, he observes, is a person who has broken down under an overload of information or a soldier who has cracked up after having been under fire too long. And those under the age of thirty, the first generation to have grown up in McLuhan's "Electric Age," seem more than any other group to be showing the strain, perhaps because they have never known anything in their lives but the relentless pressures of a supertechnological society. All of which, if one views the flight from reason with alarm, as Toffler assuredly does, doesn't augur particularly well for the future. After all, it's unlikely that, outside of rural communes, the bombardment upon the senses is apt to diminish in the next decades.

If modern society is driving millions of people literally crazy, it is also, according to some ethnologists, activating in man a number of innate and immutable animal instincts that in serener and less populated surroundings he had been able to repress. Man says Konrad Lorenz in *On Aggression,* is primarily an irrational creature, violent, hostile, and aggressive, and in joining the flight from reason, he is not running away from his essential self but, unhappily, toward it. And others —like Desmond Morris, who wrote *The Naked Ape,* and Robert Ardrey, the author of *The Territorial Imperative* —tend in general to agree with Lorenz.

All three thinkers, for example, point out that man is in some ways even more irrational than lower beings—after all, murder within a species, either in war or singly, is rare in most of the animal kingdom. When we behave irrationally and violently, these men suggest, it is the fault of the beast within us, in whom, when the pressures are on, instinct rules over reason. And, it seems, there is nothing we can do to change these instincts—we must instead change our environment by halting overpopulation. In a sense, men like Lorenz are apologists for war, murder, and madness, absolving man of guilt for aggressive and irrational behavior, and this may explain in part why their books have been so popular.

The United States, as both Toffler and Lorenz point out, isn't the only nation where unreason is on the rise, but merely the only one where it has reached epidemic proportions. The flight from reason is evident in varying degrees in Great Britain, Europe, Japan, and even Russia; in short, in all the world's advanced technological nations. ("Unreason," of course, as the Western world interprets it, has dominated over "reason" throughout history in vast portions of Asia, Africa, and the interior of South America, not to mention in primitive arctic and Pacific cultures.) And an interesting equation can be made: a greater sophistication of technology, as in the United States, equals a greater number of people turning away from reason.

A final, urgent question: is the flight from reason to be deplored, or hailed? Once again, I've discovered, the experts disagree. On the one hand there are those who view the flight from reason as a disaster to mankind in general and to the United States in particular. Says Toffler, for instance: "We are racing toward what could be the most devastating outbreak of social pathology in history." In *Madness and Civilization* Foucault saw an even more apocalyptic tendency in the sixteenth century,

which presumably might obtain today. "It is the tide of madness," he wrote, "its secret invasion, that shows that the world is near its final catastrophe; it is man's insanity that invokes and makes necessary the world's end."

On the other hand Theodore Roszak, a professor of history also writing in this issue, not only welcomes the flight from reason but views it as "the saving vision our endangered civilization requires." Modern American industrial society, says Roszak, is ugly, repressive, and destructive to the human spirit. In short, it is a nightmare society, and one that has evolved because of an automatic acceptance of the axiom that advances in science and technology are *ipso facto* good for mankind. However, says Roszak, the young are now creating a new culture in the United States, a "counter culture" that is based on unreason and aimed at liberating the nonrational forces dormant in all of us—the illogical world of our dreams and fantasies. Magic. Imagination. A sense of joy. Only by creating such a culture, he says, can we break away from the dull, deadening, and destructive domination of science and technology.

R. D. Laing, a British psychiatrist and writer, is another who applauds the flight from reason. "Madness need not be all breakdown. It may also be breakthrough. It is potentially liberation and renewal as well as enslavement and existential death," writes Laing in a book entitled *The Politics of Experience.* "The condition of alienation, of being asleep, of being unconscious, of being out of one's mind, is the condition of normal man. Society highly values its normal man. It educates children to lose themselves and to become absurd, and thus to be normal." Man, says Laing, constantly represses the natural spirit of children, as parents and teachers smother a child's innate curiosity, imagination, and illogic. "By the time the new human being is fifteen or so," writes Laing, "we are left with a being like ourselves, a half-crazed creature more or less ad-

justed to a mad world. This is normality in our present age." In consequence, since Laing, too, believes that madness is a vastly rewarding experience, he sees nothing but good in the turning away of millions from so-called normality.

So, as far as I've been able to figure out, the flight from reason is either a catastrophe or a blessing. Only the future, of course, can tell us which it really is. I can't help but hope, though, that the end-of-the-worlders are at least slightly off the mark. In any event, as the 1970's begin, a belief in the powers of unreason over reason is rapidly spreading in the United States, while science and technology are becoming increasingly suspect. Since reason has produced monsters like the war in Vietnam, a growing number of Americans are looking to the insights of madmen (or antirational mystics like Timothy Leary and the poet Allen Ginsberg) as being more relevant to life than the insights of Richard Nixon or Wernher Von Braun. In fact, for many of America's young it is only the madmen who make sense in a mad world. Truth, perhaps, lies after all not in reason but in unreason. This is the unsettling thought that has led me to wonder whether I myself, a hardnosed rationalist, might be a candidate for the flight from reason. Of course, I suspect that it will be some time before I grow a beard, don love beads, and head off to live in a rural commune. Still, I've found myself lately more and more bothered by nagging questions like this one, which I'll leave you to ponder: if, during the past thirty-five years, all the atomic physicists of the world had instead been astrologers, wouldn't we be a good deal better off today?

Thomas Meehan's latest contribution to Horizon *was "Fun Art," in the issue for Autumn, 1969. He lives amid the honeysuckles of Sherman, a small town in Connecticut, which he describes as "a very reasonable community—full of artists and writers and martini freaks."*

BEYOND REASON

A PORTFOLIO
OF PHOTOGRAPHS
BY DON SNYDER

The following portfolio was pho-
tographed for HORIZON by Don
Snyder, a young New Yorker who
spends his weekends in Stockbridge,
Massachusetts—"Alice's Restaurant"
country. These people are his friends,
or friends of friends: they are witches,
warlocks, herbalists, shamans, as-
trologists, and disciples of other
mystical practices. At right is Barry
Silverstein, known as "the Wan-
derer." In 1966 Silverstein became
concerned about the evidence he saw
of devastating water pollution caused
by a G.E. plant outside Pittsfield,
Massachusetts. Going off with half a
dozen others, he toured the country in a bus whose sides were painted
with the legend "Save the Water . . .
Save Your Children." "Everything is
together," says Silverstein—a statement ecologists often make, though
perhaps without quite the same inspiration. Temporarily off the road,
Silverstein works three days a week
as a cook at a macrobiotic restaurant, The Paradox, on East 7th Street
in New York City, where he continues somberly to spread the word.

Erica Robbins, the blithe spirit who emerges for no particular reason from behind a tombstone in a country graveyard at left, is a twenty-one-year-old pianist and dancer, trained at the Julliard School in New York. Raised in Hyannis, Massachusetts, she likes to think that her great-great-great-grandmother was burned as a heretic in Salem. Particularly enamored of spirit dances, she sometimes holds dance sessions with children in grassy meadows and hopes to go to India to study dances there. She admires Herman Hesse's *Demian* and *Siddhartha* and feels that she has the power of healing people, of foreseeing such natural events as the falling of a tree, and of communicating with animals. Her feelings about the natural world have been with her, she says, "since childhood."

Ann Carter, below, age twenty-two, is a herbalist who can read the stars and cast astrological charts. Here, she is in her own "private place" in the woods, where she has her witch's altar. Recently she traveled to British Columbia, on instructions from a spiritual source, to purchase a tract of land on an island; she now lives in Nepal.

The bells around Hetty MacLise's ankles (opposite) are "to remind me where I am." A witch who makes white, or good, magic, she is surrounded here by the accoutrements of her craft. Her altar, inside the stump of an apple tree, is bedecked with a tarot card, shells, cornmeal, a butterfly, and other objects. She holds a mink skin, and on her forehead is a pendant-symbol of the "Feet of Vishnu" or "The Incomparable Lotus Seat." Her boa-like headdress is made of cock feathers, beads, tassels, and pieces of amber and jade. She lived and studied with the Hopi Indians for a time and wears on her left hand a fire opal "power ring," given to her by the Hopi. And, for several months, she lived among a group of professional magicians in Morocco. Formerly a graphic designer for the San Francisco *Oracle*, a now-defunct underground newspaper, she currently does artwork for the *East Village Other* in New York. She is married to the poet and shaman-musician Angus MacLise (see page 16), and they have a year-old son, Ossian. Black magic is out these days, and few witches practice, or admit to practicing, magic for evil purposes. Each of Hetty MacLise's objects has been placed on her altar with a prayer; each will direct the prayer to the source of power that will bring about the desired effect: from the curing of a headache to the making of world peace.

Becca Brock, opposite, age eighteen, is the daughter of Ray Brock, the former husband of Alice. Becca dropped out of the eighth grade and has not been back to school since. Last summer she lived in these woods on a mountaintop in Stockbridge, with her animals: two sheep, three goats, five cats, three parakeets, five chickens, one horse, two donkeys, and her dog Honey. She is not a hermit: her friends come and go; the animals, with whom she communicates easily, always stay with her.

At right, Kusama and her entourage cavort at dusk atop New York's Flatiron Building, ten blocks south of the Empire State Building. Born in Tokyo, Kusama came to the United States in 1957 and over the years has enjoyed a variety of self-assumed titles: Princess of Polka Dots, High Priestess of Nudity, and Queen of Self-Obliteration. A shrewd exploiter of the media, she has staged highly publicized happenings at the New York Stock Exchange, the United Nations, and New York's Board of Elections. One of the leading exponents of group body-painting (an exercise in consciousness expansion that involves an indeterminate number of people stripping and hand-painting one another), she is a painter, a sculptress, and a fashion designer. Her fashions are designed to expose what other designers cover. One recent self-obliteration performance was promoted with broadsides reading, "Become one with eternity. Obliterate your personality. Become part of your environment. Self-destruction is the only way out." According to the late Sir Herbert Read, Kusama "creates forms that proliferate like mycelium and seal the consciousness in their white integument."

Angus MacLise grooves at right with "The Instrument," a contraption built from a barbecue pan in the image of a lyre. A music shaman, or healer, MacLise here merely fiddles at a social gathering in Stockbridge. Full trance-sessions are usually held in a marble quarry, in the meadows, or at nearby Bash Bish falls under a full moon; the call of the drum brings people together, and the nonstop music sessions "purge the evil spirits." "In ancient Greece," says MacLise, "music was the last resort in healing madness." MacLise wears a vest on which he scribbled "unknown glyphs in spontaneous writing" done in a trance.

Ann McCord, below, communes with the spirits in a swamp near her summer home in Massachusetts. Born in California, until five years ago she lived on the West Coast where she was involved in Rosicrucian activities as well as in tarot-card reading and group levitation and with the followers of Edgar Cayce, who warned that both the eastern and western coasts of America would soon fall into the sea and that Manhattan Island would drop out below 14th Street. In Massachusetts, she has designed clothes for the US dress shop in Lenox and taught at the Windsor Mountain school. A witch who practices white magic, she believes that witches' altars are "the ritualistic center for recognition of the supernatural." The significance of the embroidered cloth hanging beside her is known only to Miss McCord.

According to Hilary Harris, here in the guise of a warlock, "fun is serious." Opposite, Harris stands glumly holding an Indian drum and a rooster, both potentially magical objects. In the background are his wife, two daughters, and two towheaded children of a friend. The Thai mask (and the other tot) will be removed from the top of the carefully assembled pile of wood before it is lit and becomes the center of a ritual or a weenie roast. Harris wears a robe made for him by his wife; his necklace is made of bear claws; his forehead is held together by a beaded Indian headband. Harris is a well-known film maker. In 1962 his film *Seawards the Great Ships* won an Academy Award. He is also a sculptor; one of his recent works appeared in the autumn of 1968 in "The Machine Show" at New York's Museum of Modern Art. "The Catholic Church," says Harris, speaking of his interest in ritual, "is two hundred years behind the times. Only now they are rejecting the rituals that others are trying to regain."

Jonathan Chernoble, above, worked as a bartender, seaman, and television cameraman before he "dropped out of the death-oriented part of society." A highly articulate political activist, he runs a draft-counseling service in Pittsfield, Massachusetts. For a time he worked for the Sheffield Project in the Berkshire mountains, which aided dropouts from Harlem. Chernoble has a classical training in music and plays the trombone, cello, saxophone, flute, violin, piano, and vibes. His greatest preoccupation is nonverbal communication, whether through music, mime, touch, or noise.

In a field of Queen Anne's lace, at right, a group of boys and girls form a lotus, or star, "drawing together, to intertwine . . . to mix together . . . to become one with God and man." The participants in what is sometimes called a "group grope," insist that that rubric distorts the meaning of the event. It is not an orgy: "everyone becomes *spiritually* aroused." They are brothers and sisters.

In their flight from reason such members of the younger generation are questioning Western man's most fundamental assumptions: about the food he eats, the shelter he seeks, the clothes he wears. Here mysticism is understood to be superior to rationalism, communication by touch is found to be superior to speech, living with animals seems more rewarding than living with people, ecstasy induced by drugs or fasting or music is deemed superior to self-control. It is a child's world that many young adults seem increasingly loathe to leave.

THE MAKING OF
A COUNTER CULTURE

"... if one believes, as I do, that the alienated young are giving shape to something that looks like the saving vision our endangered civilization requires, then there is no avoiding the need to understand them"

Perhaps the best explanation of what moves the young in their flight from reason was given last fall by Theodore Roszak in his book The Making of a Counter Culture, *from which the following excerpts are taken. Mr. Roszak, thirty-seven, is associate professor of history at California State College at Hayward.*

The struggle between generations is one of the obvious constants of human affairs. One stands in peril of some presumption, therefore, in suggesting that the rivalry between young and adult in Western society during the current decade is uniquely critical. And yet it is necessary to risk such presumption if one is not to lose sight of our most important contemporary source of radical dissent and cultural innovation. For better or worse, most of what is presently happening that is new, provocative, and engaging, in politics, education, the arts, social relations (love, courtship, family, community), is the creation either of youths who are profoundly, even fanatically, alienated from the parental generation or of those who address themselves primarily to the young. It is at the level of youth that significant social criticism now looks for a responsive hearing, as more and more it grows to be the common expectation that the young should be those who act, who make things happen, who take the risks, who generally provide the ginger. It would be of interest in its own right that the age-old process of generational disaffiliation is now being transformed from a peripheral experience in the life of the individual and the family into a major lever of radical social change. But if one believes, as I do, that the alienated young are giving shape to something

that looks like the saving vision our endangered civilization requires, then there is no avoiding the need to understand them.

It would hardly seem an exaggeration to call what we see arising among the young a "counter culture." Meaning a culture so radically disaffiliated from the mainstream assumptions of our society that it scarcely looks to many like a culture at all. The interests of our college-age and adolescent young in the psychology of alienation, Oriental mysticism, psychedelic drugs, and communal experiments make for a cultural constellation that radically diverges from values and assumptions that have been in the mainstream of our society at least since the scientific revolution of the seventeenth century.

At this point the counter culture embraces only a strict minority of the young and a handful of their adult mentors. It excludes our more conservative young, for whom a bit less social security and a bit more of that old-time religion (plus more police on the beat) would be sufficient to make the Great Society a thing of beauty. It excludes our more liberal youths, for whom the alpha and omega of politics is no doubt still that Kennedy style. It excludes the scattering of old-line Marxist youth groups whose members, like their fathers before them, continue to tend the ashes of the proletarian revolution, watching for a spark to leap forth. More importantly, it excludes in large measure the militant black young, whose political activity has become so narrowly defined in ethnic terms that, despite its urgency, it has become for the time being as culturally old-fashioned as the nationalist mythopoesis of the nineteenth century.

If there is any justification for such exceptions in a discussion of youth, it must be that the counter-cultural young are significant enough both in numbers and in critical force to merit independent attention. But from my own point of view the counter culture, far more than merely "meriting" attention, desperately requires it, since I am at a loss to know where, besides among these dissenting young people and their heirs of the next few generations, the radical discontent and innovation can be found that might transform this disoriented civilization of ours into something a human being can identify as home. They are the matrix in which an alternative, but still excessively fragile, future is taking shape. Granted, that alternative comes dressed in a garish motley borrowed from many and exotic sources—from depth psychiatry, from the mellowed remnants of left-wing ideology, from the Oriental religions, from romantic Weltschmerz, from anarchist social theory, from Dada and American Indian lore, and I suppose, from the perennial wisdom. Still, the alternative looks to me like all we have to hold against the final consolidation of a technocracy in which we shall find ourselves ingeniously adapted to an existence wholly estranged from everything that has ever made the life of man an interesting adventure.

By technocracy I mean that social form in which an industrial society reaches the peak of its organizational integration. It is the ideal men usually have in mind when they speak of modernizing, updating, rationalizing, planning. The meticulous systematization Adam Smith once celebrated in his well-known pin factory now extends to all areas of life, giving us a human

By THEODORE ROSZAK

organization that matches the precision of our mechanistic organization. So we arrive at the era of social engineering in which entrepreneurial talent broadens its province to orchestrate the total human context that surrounds the industrial complex. Politics, education, leisure, entertainment, culture as a whole, the unconscious drives, even protest against the technocracy itself: all these become the subjects of purely technical scrutiny and of purely technical manipulation.

How marvelously the assimilative capacities of the technocracy beguile and mislead! As the educational level of the Great Society rises, we all assume a veneer of eclectic cultural polish. We decorate our lives with good music stations and expensive reproductions of the old masters, with shelves of paperback classics and extension courses in comparative religions. Perhaps we go on to dabble in water colors or the classical guitar, flower arranging or a bit of amateur yoga. Higher education, tamed and integrated into the needs of the technocracy, treats us to magisterial surveys of great art and thought in order that we might learn how not to be boors—as befits a society of imperial affluence. The senatorial classes of ancient Rome sent their scions touring the schools of Athens; the American middle class processes its young through the multiversity. Another generation and surely our corridors of power will sparkle with the best conversation in the land. We have already had the taste of a President who could festoon his every speech with learned allusions and a secretary of defense who could quote Aristotle.

But these adventures in sophistication are viciously subversive. They allow us to throw off flurries of intellectual sparks, but short-circuit any deeper level of the personality. They teach us appreciative gestures, but avoid the white-hot experience of authentic vision that might transform our lives, and in so doing, set us at warlike odds with the dominant culture. To achieve such 'a shattering transformation of the personality, *one* poem by Blake, *one* canvas by Rembrandt, *one* Buddhist sutra might be enough . . . were we but opened to the power of the word, the image, the presence before us. When such an upheaval of the personality happens, our dissenting young show us the result. They drop out! The multiversity loses them; the society loses them. They go over to the counter culture. And then the concerned parents, the administrators, and the technocrats wag their heads dolefully and ask, "Where have we failed our youth?" Meaning: "How have we made the mistake of producing children who take with such desperate seriousness what was only intended as a little cultural savvy?"

The strange youngsters who don cowbells and primitive talismans, who take to the public parks or the wilderness to improvise outlandish communal ceremonies, are in reality seeking to ground democracy safely beyond the culture of expertise. They give us back the image of the Paleolithic band, where the community during its rituals stood in the presence of the sacred in a rude equality that predated class, state, and status. It is a strange brand of radicalism we have here that turns to prehistoric precedent for its inspiration.

If the resistance of the counter culture fails, I think there will be nothing in store for us but what anti-utopians like Huxley and Orwell have forecast —though I have no doubt that these dismal despotisms will be far more stable and effective than their· prophets have foreseen. For they will be equipped with techniques of inner-manipulation as unobtrusively fine as gossamer. The capacity of our emerging technocratic paradise to denature the imagination by appropriating to itself the whole meaning of Reason, Reality, Progress, and Knowledge will render it impossible for men to give any name to their bothersomely unfulfilled potentialities but that of madness. And for such madness, humanitarian therapies will be generously provided.

It is not easy to question the thoroughly sensible, thoroughly well-intentioned but nevertheless reductive humanism with which the technocracy surrounds itself, without seeming to speak a dead and discredited language. Especially so if one admits—as I do (*pace* the doctrinaire eschatology of the old and new left)—that it may well lie within the capability of the technocracy to utilize its industrial prowess, its social engineering, its sheer affluence, and its well-developed diversionary tactics in order to reduce, in ways that most people will find perfectly acceptable, all the tensions born of the disorganization, privation, and injustice that currently unsettle our lives. (Note that I do not say it will *solve* the problems; but rather, like adjustive psychotherapy, it will cunningly soothe the neurotic hurt.) The technocracy is not simply a power structure wielding vast material influence; it is the expression of a grand cultural imperative, a veritable mystique that is deeply endorsed by the populace. It is therefore a capacious sponge, able to soak up prodigious quantities of discontent and agitation, often long before they look like anything but amusing eccentricities or uncalled-for aberrations. The question therefore arises, if the technocracy in its grand procession through history is indeed pursuing to the satisfaction of so many such universally ratified values as The Quest for Truth, The Conquest of Nature, The Abundant Society, The Creative Leisure, The Well-Adjusted Life, why not settle back and enjoy the trip?

The answer is, I guess, that I find myself unable to see anything at the end of the road we are following with such self-assured momentum but Samuel Beckett's two sad tramps forever waiting under that wilted tree for their lives to begin. Except that I think the tree isn't going to be real, but rather, a plastic counterfeit. In fact, even the tramps may turn out to be automatons . . . though of course there will be great, programmed grins on their faces.

FROM THE BOOK *The Making of a Counter Culture* BY THEODORE ROSZAK. COPYRIGHT © 1969 BY THEODORE ROSZAK. PUBLISHED BY DOUBLEDAY & COMPANY, INC.

THE DESERT HERMITS

"If you had asked a citizen of the Christian Roman Empire whether the anchorites and stylites were performing any valuable function by withdrawing from society, he would have replied that by withdrawing from it they were saving it"

By ARNOLD J. TOYNBEE

Has rationality ever, at any time or place, had the upper hand over irrational beliefs and feelings and behavior? If you put this question to a moderately well educated present-day Westerner, his answer is likely to be that he can think of two such cases: the Greek world from the sixth to about the second century B.C., and the modern Western world since the end of the seventeenth century. In the former case he will perhaps remember that "the decline and fall" that is the subject of Gibbon's history is the miscarriage not just of the Roman Empire but of the "rational" Greco-Roman civilization that the Roman Empire had incapsulated in the latest stage of its history. Greco-Roman rationality did decline and fall; Gibbon himself summed up his work by saying that he had described "the triumph of barbarism and

religion." The present-day Westerner may perhaps have a disquieting suspicion that since the outbreak of the First World War, our modern civilization has entered on the same fatal course.

In the late Greco-Roman world one of the dramatic signs of collapse was the withdrawal from society of individuals who found that society dissatisfying and disgusting. The earliest Christian anchorites (withdrawers) were Egyptians who withdrew from the thickly populated Nile valley into the adjoining desert. There were other Christian ascetics who withdrew vertically instead of horizontally. Stylites, or pillar men, perched, for years on end, on the tops of columns. These withdrawals, for the purpose of practicing extreme self-mortification, spiritual and mental, seemed to Gibbon, in

retrospect, to be inexplicably and distastefully irrational. If the anchorites' and stylites' performances could have been foreseen by Pericles or by Aristotle, no doubt they would have reacted as Gibbon did. In order to understand the anchorites' behavior, we have to see it as a response to the moral failure of the world of Pericles and Aristotle.

The prelude to Christian asceticism was a centuries-long series of disillusioning shocks. The first of these was the self-destruction of the Greek city-states in round after round of fratricidal wars that began with the outbreak of the great Peloponnesian War in 431 B.C. (Pericles himself was largely responsible for this catastrophe.) The second shock was the subjugation of the enfeebled Greek city-states by the most backward of all the Greek peo-

The Thebaïd, a fourteenth-century painting attributed to Gherardo Starnina, depicts the Egyptian desert around Thebes as teeming with anchorites. The body of Saint Paul, the first Christian hermit and a contemporary of Saint Anthony, is shown in repose at far left, surrounded by mourners. The monk whose cart is pulled by a team of lions (seen to the left of the monastery garden) may be Saint Jerome or Saint Anthony on his way to bury Saint Paul. To the right of center a beautiful girl has attempted to seduce a hermit who sits in front of one of the topmost huts; unsuccessful, she flees, unsheathing the demonic claws that reveal her true origin.

ples, the Macedonians. The third shock was the sudden, premature death of Alexander the Great in 323 B.C., which was followed by another round of wars between his generals over dividing the spoils of the Persian Empire. The fourth shock—and this was the worst one yet

23

—was the two centuries of agony that began in 218 B.C. with the outbreak of the Second Punic War between Rome and Carthage and that ended at last, when in 31 B.C. Augustus imposed peace on all the countries round the shores of the Mediterranean. The last straw was the breakdown, in the third century of the Christian Era, of the law and order that had been established temporarily by Augustus.

The effect of these successive shocks showed itself first in Greek philosophy. The sixth century B.C., in which Greek philosophy began, was an age of confidence in the Greek world, and the Greek philosophers of that age studied the material structure of the cosmos. Their chief concerns were physics and astronomy. Socrates, who was a contemporary of Pericles and of "the beginning of great evils" for the Greek world, deliberately turned away from physical science to ethics. In the Greek world, by Socrates' time, human relations had gone wrong conspicuously and painfully enough to claim a philosopher's undivided attention. Socrates became a moral philosopher, but he remained a rationalist. Socrates believed that human wickedness was due to ignorance, and that if a human being saw the truth, he would do what was right—a belief that is contradicted by everyone's daily experience of his neighbors' behavior and his own.

No such faith in reason moved the Christian ascetics of the later Roman Empire. Their reaction to the breakdown of Greco-Roman society showed itself in a consciousness of sin—the individual's personal sinfulness and the congenital sinfulness of all mankind. Turning their backs on the wickedness of the world, they sought redemption by the infliction of suffering on themselves. They could no longer have themselves put to death, like the early Christian martyrs, by Roman public authorities, for these had now become their coreligionists; but they could shorten their lives by self-imposed austerities and could meanwhile torment themselves mentally as well as physically. In their cells and on their pillars they were afflicted, not surprisingly, by psychic tortures and temptations that they interpreted as being the physical assaults of demons.

The two fathers of Christian asceticism were both Egyptians of the fourth century. Saint Anthony, the father of solitary anchoritism, died in the year 356; Saint Pachomius, the father of monasticism in the form of an ascetic community, lived from about 286 to 346. Saint Anthony was not the earliest Christian anchorite. Paul of Thebes had withdrawn to the desert a generation earlier. It was, however, Saint Anthony who made the fortunes of anchoritism by gaining the attention and admiration of the public. People who did not already know of him by hearsay could read an arresting account of his life that appeared in Greek about the year 357 and that is said to have been written by Saint Athanasius, the celebrated church father who was Patriarch of Alexandria. It was Saint Anthony's fame that moved thousands to follow him into the desert, tens of thousands to make pilgrimages to the haunts of these desert fathers, and millions to feel an emotional attachment to the heroic spiritual athletes whom ordinary mortals could not aspire to emulate.

The solitary and the social forms of asceticism had two fundamental practices in common: withdrawal from the secular world and doing work. This work was done, not for its own sake, but for its spiritual value. The ascetics preferred simple work of a mechanical kind—plaiting baskets or weaving mats—which, not unlike the tending of machines in a modern factory, left the worker's mind free to think about other things. The sale of the ascetics' wares enabled them to earn their livings; the production of these wares helped them to preserve their sanity—and this was one of the necessities of the ascetic life, for asceticism has a built-in tendency to go to ever further extremes, especially when the ascetic is living a solitary life and has to be his own spiritual disciplinarian.

The regime that these ascetics imposed on themselves was indeed severe. They worked throughout the day without speaking and without eating. They woke themselves up at midnight for prayer and meditation. They then kept themselves awake till dawn, and it was in the small hours that they were assailed by demons—in imagination, we should suppose today, but in corporeal reality as the ascetics interpreted their own experience. Their reports of these encounters with demons were heard and read with eagerness and enthusiasm. The desert fathers' fame sprang largely from their prowess in resisting and overcoming their real or imaginary diabolical adversaries.

They were, however, on their guard against tormenting themselves to the point of diminishing spiritual returns. "Excessive fasts have the same untoward effects as gluttony," remarked John Cassian, and he was writing from experience. He had been a monk in Egypt for fifteen years toward the close of the fourth century, and he afterward founded, on the French Riviera, the first monastery in western Europe. Cassian lists eight vices against which the ascetic ought to be on his guard. They are gluttony, impurity, avarice, anger, melancholy, listlessness, vainglory, and pride.

The warning was timely, for in Syria, in contrast to Egypt, the ascetics certainly did go to extremes. It was common form for Syrian ascetics to wear chains, but one of them thought of chaining himself in a way that forced him to walk on all fours. A shepherd mistook him for a wolf and nearly killed him with a slingstone. Another allowed himself to be buried so deep under a fall of snow that he had to be dug out. Another lived in a cabin in which the roof was too low to allow him to stand upright, but this was not sufficient discomfort to satisfy him, so he took to walking, with his hands up, enveloped in a leather bag with slits for his nostrils and his mouth (but not his

"Let no one who hath renounced the world think that he hath given up some great thing." So said Saint Anthony, the founding father of solitary anchoritism and a source of inspiration to painters down the ages. Sassetta's *St. Anthony Tormented by Demons*, a detail of which is at left, is one of numerous fifteenth-century works showing the saint abused by monsters. Anthony was born in Egypt around A.D. 251, the son of a prosperous Christian farming family. His parents died when he was twenty, leaving him an estate and a younger sister to look after. But then came the crisis of his life: in church one Sunday he heard his priest read Jesus' exhortation, "Go, sell what you possess and give to the poor." Overwhelmed, Anthony at once obeyed. Having provided for his sister, he turned his back on the world as he knew it and set off for the desert. Hunger and solitude and sand have long been known to engender phantasmagoria, and Anthony was visited by a host of fiends. The gods of ancient Egypt came to mock him. The devil planted lovely naked girls under every bush and otherwise plumbed the repertory of hellish erotica. Snakes and scorpions, demons and dragons, arrived from out of nowhere. The tormented saint withstood it all, the enticing as well as the horrifying.

After twenty years Anthony emerged to find a group of disciples awaiting him. Together they founded a community of hermits, but after several years as its abbot, Anthony retreated to the desert again; he died there at the age of one hundred and five. By the end of the fourth century the number of hermits in the Egyptian desert was said to equal the population of the towns. Unnatural though they must have seemed to the world they had repudiated, their tradition has lasted even into our own day.

YALE UNIVERSITY ART GALLERY, JAMES JACKSON JARVES COLL.

A pair of demons harass Saint Anthony in the desert.

eyes). Another made for himself a contraption like the treadmill in a squirrel's cage. But the Syrian ascetics' special invention was standing on the tops of pillars. The Syrian stylites became superlatively famous, and this form of self-torment spread from Syria to Asia Minor, Constantinople, and Salonica, where the winters are harsh indeed.

Even in Syria these extravagances were probably exceptional. They were surely exhibitions of at least three of the ascetics' besetting sins, namely gluttony (for discomfort), vainglory, and pride. Unfortunately these exhibitionists, who in truth were less edifying than their more temperate Egyptian brethren, caught the public's imagination, but it is perhaps also significant that there are no stylites today, whereas the more moderate forms of Christian asceticism are still being practiced.

A rationalist will raise the question of whether the ascetics were making a useful contribution to the cure of the Greco-Roman society's grievous spiritual sickness. Had not the Roman emperors Augustus and Marcus Aurelius and Diocletian led more useful lives? Augustus had spent himself, during the second chapter of his career, by putting an end to an anarchy that had brought the Greco-Roman society to the verge of self-destruction. Marcus Aurelius had borne patiently the almost intolerable burden of keeping in order the world that Augustus had bequeathed to his successors. Diocletian had undertaken the still more thankless task of putting the Roman Empire together again after it had lapsed into a fresh bout of anarchy that had lasted fifty years. Augustus and Diocletian had been ruthless sinners who had re-

pented only after their sins had carried them to the political summit. But Marcus Aurelius had been a pagan saint. Had not these three emperors—and many less distinguished Roman administrators as well—performed better services for society than the Christian ascetics? How was it, then, that the ascetics were able to arouse a mass enthusiasm that even the greatest and best of the Roman emperors failed to evoke?

The ascetics moved the hearts of their contemporaries—and of posterity, too—because they gave sensational expression to the prevalent mood of their age. They had the strength of mind and body to achieve what all the Christian world was then trying to achieve. They did this vicariously for their fellow human beings, and so they won their weaker brethren's fervent

25

"A swarm of fanatics, incapable of fear, or reason, or humanity . . ." When Gibbon wrote this description of the Eastern ascetics, he may have been thinking of Simeon Stylites, who achieved sainthood by spending thirty-seven years atop a pillar in the Syrian Desert. The sixth-century silver plaque at left commemorates the feat. Gibbon's reaction to the "fanatics" is that of a completely rational mind to its opposite number. Simeon was born in Syria about A.D. 390 and became a devout Christian. He entered a monastery as a youth, where his feats of self-abnegation became the envy of his brethren. Once he buried himself up to his armpits and refused to move for two years. He accomplished prodigious fasts. One day he bound a rope so tightly around his waist that the flesh putrefied and a surgeon had to be called. This act of extremism disgusted the other monks, and the abbot invited Simeon to depart. He became a desert hermit, but like many another who has scorned the world, he was soon besieged by supplicants in need of counsel. Simeon therefore built himself a pillar, which eventually was raised to a height of sixty feet. He chained himself to the pinnacle and stayed there the rest of his life, unmindful of the burning sun, his ulcerated legs, his multitudinous vermin, and the admiring crowds below.

Why? Perhaps he was a lunatic, as Gibbon would have thought. Or perhaps he belonged to some heretical Oriental Christian sect. Or perhaps he had heard about the nearby temple of Aphrodite at Hierapolis, the high priest of which spent seven days each year perched atop a gigantic sculptured phallus. That was his way of drawing closer to his goddess. Simeon may only have been using the same method to draw closer to his own deity.

Saint Simeon on his pillar resists the devilish wiles of a snake.

admiration and gratitude. If you had asked a citizen of the Christian Roman Empire whether the anchorites and stylites were performing any valuable function by withdrawing from society, he would have replied that by withdrawing from it they were saving it.

The fame and popularity that the ascetics' austerities won for them were no less characteristic of their careers than the austerities themselves. Visit, as I have done, the stump (authentic or faked) of the column in northern Syria that Saint Simeon Stylites lived on for thirty-seven years (A.D. 422–459). The stump is enshrined in a church that is magnificent even in its present state of ruin, and the church, with the monastery attaching to it, is supplemented, at the foot of the hill, by the ruins of a cluster of hostels for pilgrims that amount to a veritable city. Visit San

Giovanni Rotondo on the spur of Italy, or Fátima in Portugal: in both these holy places of the present-day Catholic Western world you will find contemporary counterparts of the ruined hostels that lie at the foot of Saint Simeon's hill.

These Christian ascetics were, indeed, quite as popular and as famous as contemporary public entertainers: star drivers of racing chariots, dancers, wrestlers, boxers, and the rest. Moreover, the ascetics' fame has lasted much longer. We may know the names of some of the entertainers, but we do not know much else about them. The contemporary ascetics fared better. Admirers wrote their lives, and these biographies, part fact and part fiction, were copied and recopied till eventually they got into print. They are still extant; we can read them today.

The fame of the Egyptian ascetics is particularly striking, for in the pre-Christian Roman Empire the native Egyptians had been on the lowest rung of the political and social ladder. The citizens and subjects of the pre-Christian Roman Empire were marshaled in a hierarchy in which the Egyptians ranked lowest of all. The Romans looked down on the Greeks; the Egyptian Greeks—the Greeks of Alexandria, for instance—looked down on the Egyptian natives. And then, suddenly, Egypt became the Greek and Roman pagans' holy land, and the Christian Egyptian ascetics became the Christian Greco-Roman world's heroes.

In truth, these Christian ascetics were not indifferent to the sins and sufferings of the world from which they had withdrawn physically. They not only prayed for the salvation of mankind; occasionally they intervened actively in politics. One stylite, whose column was within reach of the Christian empire's capital, Constantinople, once brought an emperor to his knees by threatening to come down to earth and eventually carrying out his threat and confronting the emperor in his palace. The emperor had to capitulate. If he had defied the stylite, and still more if he had touched one hair of his head, he would have been swept off his throne by the torrent of indignant public feeling.

The anchorites were eventually defeated not by the public authorities but by their own popularity. The ruined hostels below Saint Simeon's column and church tell the tale. The ascetics inspired multitudes to follow their example, and far greater multitudes to show their admiration by going on pilgrimages to witness the ascetics' feats. The dominant personalities among the ascetics found themselves compelled to organize their fellow monks into communities living a corporate life under written codes of disciplinary rules. The Greek word *monakhos*, from which the English word "monk" derives, means solitary, and a monastery is literally "a community of solitaries." This is a contradiction in terms, and it illustrates the impossibility of anchoritism as a permanent way of life.

Both anchoritism and corporate monasticism spread like wildfire through the Christian world. During the Middle Ages the monasteries were the most efficiently managed of all institutions—better managed than any medieval states or private business enterprises. Visit the ruins of the Cistercian monasteries in the Cleveland Hills in Yorkshire. The story of the monks can hold its own against the epic of the North American pioneers. These monks tamed the wilderness; they exploited its pastoral and mineral wealth, and they built up industries that became so prosperous that covetous hands engineered the dissolution

of the monasteries in England in the sixteenth century.

Thus, in the history of Christian monasticism, the anchorites' success had an ironic sequel. The admiration they had won by withdrawing from the wicked world eventually drew them back into this wicked world. Their corporate discipline and their relatively high level of education and conduct made the economic fortunes of the anchorites' offspring, the monastic communities. This corporate economic prosperity made the monks worldly-minded. They became hard bargainers and harsh landlords. In England, by the time of King Henry VIII, some monasteries had become rich enough to make it worthwhile for the Crown to dissolve them and seize their property. The earlier King Henrys could not have ventured to commit this tempting act of lucrative spoliation. They would have outraged public opinion to a perilous degree. Henry VIII judged that the monasteries' moral stock had depreciated to a level at which he could expropriate their great possessions with impunity, and the event proved that his calculation had been correct. Thus in the course of thirteen centuries, running from Saint Anthony's generation to Henry VIII's, the history of monasticism had come full circle.

In our own troubled times we may look back at the anchorites with a new understanding. In our world, as in the Greco-Roman world, people with pride in a rational order of society have been overtaken by a revolt against rationality that they did not expect and have not been able to understand. The rationalists' expectations have been disappointed for two reasons. The first reason is that our civilization—as was true of the Greco-Roman civilization—is not as rational as the rationalists supposed. It is rational in its science and technology, but not rational in the uses it has made of the intellectual and practical achievements of rational pursuits. In both cases science and technology have been used for human pur-

poses that are irrational, antisocial, immoral, and spiritually abject. In our own time the discovery of the structure of the atom was a triumph of science; the discovery of devices for releasing the energy latent in this structure was a triumph of technology. But the principal use to which these triumphs of the human reason have been put so far has been the manufacture of weapons that might destroy the user as well as his victim and might possibly even destroy all life on this planet. We know this, yet we persist in the competitive production of more and more deadly atomic weapons, and biological weapons, too. And what could be more irrational than that?

Bitter, disillusioning experience has taught the victims of it that rationality is not enough. The fruits of rationality can be misused for the pursuit of wicked and disastrous objectives. This is one of the reasons for the violent revulsion against rationality in our day, and it was one of the reasons for it in the last chapter of the history of the Greco-Roman world.

The other, deeper reason for the revolt is the realization that rationality is not the most important ingredient in human behavior, and here the rebels have made the tragic mistake of seeking an antidote to the failure of rationality by cultivating irrationality for its own sake. They have tended to cultivate it in the form of gross and sterile superstition. What they ought to have done was not to have jettisoned rationality but to have dedicated themselves to love. Mankind's right spiritual guides are not the Christian ascetics but the Buddha, Jesus, and Francis of Assisi, each of whom scandalized his ascetic-minded contemporaries by the discovery, through personal experience, that love, not asceticism, is the true end of man—and by the application of this truth to his relations with his fellow human beings.

The most renowned of living historians, Arnold J. Toynbee is best known for his classic multivolumed Study of History.

Why They Read Hesse

"Curiously, a man who spoke for my father's generation is now heard loud and clear by my sons and daughters"

By KURT VONNEGUT, JR.

Here are the bare bones of a tale that will always be popular with the young anywhere. A man travels a lot, is often alone. Money is not a serious problem. He seeks spiritual comfort, and avoids marriage and boring work. He is more intelligent than his parents and most of the people he meets. Women like him. So do poor people. So do wise old men. He experiments with sex, finds it nice but not tremendous. He encounters many queerly lovely hints that spiritual comfort really can be found. The world is beautiful. There is magic around.

The story has everything but novelty. Chrétien de Troyes had success with it eight hundred years ago, in *Perceval le Gallois*. He had Perceval hunt for the Holy Grail, the cup Christ used at the Last Supper. Jack Kerouac and J. D. Salinger and Saul Bellow, among others, have been admired in recent times for their tales of quests.

But the modern man who told them best was Hermann Hesse. He has been dead for eight years now. He was about my father's age. He was a German, and later a Swiss. He is deeply loved by those among the American young who are questing.

His simplest, clearest, most innocent tale of seeking and finding is *Siddhartha* (1922). How popular is it? Nearly one million copies have been printed in America since 1957. One quarter of

Hermann Hesse, seated between his young son Bruno and a companion, was on an outing in southern Switzerland when this photograph was taken by another son, Martin. The time is probably about 1915. Hesse left his native Germany in 1912, never to return.

those were sold last year. This year is expected to be even better.

Hesse is no black humorist. Black humorists' holy wanderers find nothing but junk and lies and idiocy wherever they go. A chewing-gum wrapper or a used condom is often the best they can do for a Holy Grail. Not so with the wanderers of Hesse; they always find something satisfying—holiness, wisdom, hope. Here are some Hesse endings to enjoy:

"Perhaps . . . I will turn out to be a poet after all. This would mean as much, or perhaps more, to me than being a village councilor—or the builder of the stone dams. Yet it could never mean as much to me . . . as the memory of all those beloved people, from slender Rösi Girtanner to poor Boppi." (*Peter Camenzind*, 1904.)

"Govinda bowed low. Incontrollable tears trickled down his old face. He was overwhelmed by a feeling of great love, of the most humble veneration. He bowed low, right down to the ground, in front of the man sitting there motionless, whose smile reminded him of everything that he had ever loved in his life, of everything that had ever been of value and holy in his life." (*Siddhartha*.)

"I understood it all. I understood Pablo. I understood Mozart, and somewhere behind me I heard his ghastly laughter. I knew that all the hundred thousand pieces of life's game were in my pocket. A glimpse of its meaning had stirred my reason, and I was determined to begin the game afresh. . . . One day I would be a better hand at the game. One day I would learn how to laugh. Pablo was waiting for me,

and Mozart, too." (*Steppenwolf*, 1927.)

"Dressing the wound hurt. Everything that has happened to me since has hurt. But sometimes when I find the key and climb deep into myself where the images of fate lie aslumber in the dark mirror, I need only bend over that dark mirror to behold my own image, now completely resembling him, my brother, my master." (*Demian*, 1925.)

Lovely. Hesse has had sensitive, truly bilingual English translators, by the way—Michael Roloff and Hilda Rosner and Ursule Molinaro among them.

So an easy explanation of American youth's love for Hesse is this: he is clear and direct and well translated, and he offers hope and romance, which the young play hell finding anywhere else these days. And that is such a *sunny* explanation.

But there are darker, deeper explanations to be found—and the clue that they exist is that the most important Hesse book to the American young, by their own account, is the wholly Germanic, hopelessly dated jumble called *Steppenwolf*.

Students of the famous Generation Gap might ponder this: two of the leading characters in *Steppenwolf* are Johann Wolfgang von Goethe (1749–1832) and Wolfgang Amadeus Mozart (1756–1791), who appear as ghosts in dreams.

And here is a sample of dated dialogue, which the young do not choose to laugh at:

The lonely hero, Harry Haller, has picked up a girl in a dance hall, and she says, "Now we'll go and give your shoes and trousers a brush and then you'll dance the shimmy with me."

And he replies, "I can dance no shimmy, nor waltz, nor polka, nor any of the rest of them."

Twenty-three skiddoo!

The mere title *Steppenwolf* (a wolf of the steppes) has magic. I can see a lonesome freshman, coming from a gas-station community to a great university, can see him roaming the big bookstore for the first time. He leaves with a small paper bag containing the first serious book he has ever bought for himself: hey presto! *Steppenwolf!*

He has nice clothes and a little money, but he is depressed and leery of women. When he reads *Steppenwolf* in his dismal room, so far from home and mother, he will find that it is about a middle-aged man in a dismal room, far from home and mother. This man has nice clothes and a little money, but he is depressed and leery of women.

I recently asked a young drummer, a dropout from the University of Iowa and an admirer of *Steppenwolf*, why he thought the book was selling so well. I told him an astonishing fact: Bantam Books brought out a dollar-and-a-quarter edition of *Steppenwolf* in September of last year and sold 360,000 copies in thirty days.

The drummer said that most college people were experimenting with drugs and that *Steppenwolf* harmonized perfectly with their experiences.

"I thought the best part of the drug experience was that *everything* harmonized with it—everything but the police department," I said.

The drummer admitted this was so.

I suggested to him that America teemed with people who were homesick in bittersweet ways, and that *Steppenwolf* was the most profound book about homesickness ever written.

Characters in *Steppenwolf* do use drugs from time to time, it's true—a pinch of laudanum (tincture of opium) or a sniff of cocaine now and then to chase the blues. A jazz musician gives the hero a yellow cigarette that induces fantastic dreams. But the drugs are

never adored, or feared either. They are simply medicines that friends pass around. Nobody is hooked, and nobody argues that drugs are the key to anything important.

Nor have I found Hesse to be tantalized by the drug experience in his other books. He is more concerned with alcohol. Again and again, his holy wanderers love wine too much. They do something about it, too. They resolve to keep out of taverns, though they miss the uncritical companionship they've had there.

The politics espoused by the hero of *Steppenwolf* coincide with those of the American young, all right: he is against war. He hates armament manufacturers and super-patriots. No nations or political figures or historical events are investigated or praised or blamed. There are no daring schemes, no calls to action, nothing to make a radical's heart beat faster.

Hesse shocks and thrills the American young by taking them on a lunatic's tour of a splendid nightmare—down endless corridors, through halls of breaking mirrors, to costume balls, to empty theatres showing grotesque plays and films, to a wall with a thousand doors in it, and on and on. A sign appears once in an alley, fades forever. Sinister strangers hand the hero curious messages. And on and on.

A magic theatre fantasy in which Harry Haller takes part proves, incidentally, that Hesse might have been one of the most screamingly funny men of his time. It may be that he was so anguished as he wrote *Steppenwolf* that his soul could get relief only by erupting into Charlie Chaplin comedy. The fantasy is about two men who climb a tree by a road. They have a rifle. They declare war on all automobiles and shoot them as they come by.

I laughed. There aren't many laughs in the works of Hermann Hesse. This is because romances work only if all the characters take life very seriously.

Steppenwolf is a Hesse freak for including a comedy—and a freak again for acknowledging modern technology

and hating it, by and large. Most of his tales take place in villages and countrysides, often before the First World War. No internal-combustion engine ever shatters the silence. No telephone rings. No news comes from a radio. Messages are delivered by hand, or in the voices of a river or a wind.

Nobody in *Steppenwolf* has a telephone, although the cast is in a rich city after the war, doing the shimmy to jazz. The hero has no radio in his room, despite his swooning loneliness, but there are radios around, because he dreams of listening to one in the company of Mozart. The Concerto Grosso in F major, by Handel, is being broadcast from Munich. The hero says this about it, marvelously: "the devilish tin trumpet spat out, without more ado, a mixture of bronchial slime and chewed rubber; that noise that owners of gramophones and radios have agreed to call music."

I have said that Hesse was about the same age as my father. My father wasn't a European, but part of his education took place in Strasbourg—before the First World War. And when I got to know him, when Hesse was writing *Steppenwolf*, my father, too, was cursing radios and films, was dreaming of Mozart and Goethe, was itching to pot shot automobiles.

Curiously, Hesse, a man who spoke for my father's generation, is now heard loud and clear by my daughters and sons.

And I say again: what my daughters and sons are responding to in *Steppenwolf* is the homesickness of the author. I do not mock homesickness as a silly affliction that is soon outgrown. I never outgrew it and neither did my father and neither did Hesse. I miss my Mommy and Daddy, and I always will—because they were so nice to me. Now and then, I would like to be a child again.

And who am I when I spend a night alone in a motel outside, say, Erie, Pennsylvania? Who am I when I prowl that room, find only trash on tele-

This silhouette of Hesse reading was made at the villa on the German shore of Lake Constance to which he moved in 1904.

vision, when I search the phone book for nonexistent friends and relatives in Erie? Who am I when I think of going to a cocktail lounge for the easy comradeship there, when I imagine meeting a friendly woman out there and dread the kind of woman I would be likely to meet? I am Steppenwolf.

The man who calls himself Steppenwolf, by the way, is one of the least carnivorous characters in fiction. He is a fool and a prig and a coward. He is a lamb.

Hesse's German parents hoped, when he was a boy, that he would become a minister. But he suffered a severe religious crisis when he was fourteen. He ran away from the seminary, tried suicide by and by. In *Beneath the Wheel* (1906), the only Hesse book I've read that has a hopelessly unhappy ending, he shows himself as an abused schoolboy who gets drunk and drowns.

He published his first book, *Peter Camenzind*, when he was twenty-seven. It was extremely popular in Germany. Hesse continued to prosper in his native land, and then, in 1912 when he was thirty-five, he left Germany forever. He eventually went to Switzerland.

He removed himself from Kaiser Wilhelm's shrill militarism, Hitler, two lost world wars, the partitioning of Germany, and all that. And all that. While his former countrymen were dying and killing in the trenches, Hermann Hesse was being psychoanalyzed by Carl Jung in a multilingual peaceful little land. He published romantic novels and poetry, traveled to the Far East. He was married three times.

In 1946, one year after the death of Hitler, he received the Goethe Prize. He won a handsomely deserved Nobel Prize a year after that—not as a German but as a Swiss. He wasn't representing a German culture that was rising from the ashes. He was representing a culture that had cleared the hell out of Germany just before the holocaust began.

This is something a lot of young Americans are considering, too—clearing out before a holocaust begins. Much luck to them. Their problem is this: the next holocaust will leave this planet uninhabitable, and the Moon is no Switzerland. Neither is Venus. Neither is Mars. In all the rest of the solar system, there is nothing to breathe. Not only would *Steppenwolf* be homesick on some other planet. He would die.

Kurt Vonnegut, Jr., is the author of Cat's Cradle, Slaughterhouse-Five, *and several other novels that have made him a cult hero who equals or surpasses Hermann Hesse in popularity. He resides on Cape Cod with his wife and live-in cult of six children and a large sheep dog.*

Halfway to 1984

Orwell's classic dystopia remains the bugaboo of our century: the ultimate in rationalism gone mad. Here is a reassessment of the author and his work and a guess at how close we are to living down to his vision

I never think of 1984, either the book or the year, without a slight shudder of foreboding. This can be no accidental idiosyncrasy. George Orwell set out to shock by the juxtaposition of fact and fancy. He combined the stylistic skills of the modern polemicist with the wry detachment of the classical moralist. He stood the year of the book's completion on its head to sum up his negative vision of the future in a single stroke. He had considered entitling it *The Last Man in Europe*, which lacks the stinging immediacy of his final choice but gives a stronger clue to his humanist aspirations. Had he been less a propagandist (and he said every artist was a propagandist for his own vision of life), I would not be writing this now. This curious, uncomfortably honest, and painfully decent man wanted to reach his readers primarily for political purposes; by the end of his life as a writer he had come to believe that people didn't make aesthetic judgments at all, only political ones. He wanted to be a popular author without surrendering his particular vision of the world. In all this he succeeded. Since World War II no political book, whether fiction or nonfiction—and the essence of Orwell's success is that no one is ever sure whether *1984* is one or the other—has passed more thoroughly into the English language and the popu-

Juan Genovés's Beyond the Limit *might serve as a visual metaphor for an Orwellian nightmare in which an all-seeing eye obliterates any hope of privacy or individuality.*

lar consciousness of the Western world than Orwell's dark masterpiece.

Various insights expressed in this short, prophetic tract (Orwell described it as "a Utopia in the form of a novel") have secured a hold on individuals and groups of amazing diversity. *Life* published the first excerpts in 1949 with cartoon illustrations by Abner Dean; readers were offered the interpretation

George Orwell, 1943

that "in the year 1984 left-wing totalitarianism rules the world." Michael Harrington wrote that Orwell had discovered that a technology of abundance would disenfranchise the victims of poverty and racism to maintain a permanent menial class. The John Birch Society of Westchester County offered *1984* for sale, and its Washington branch adopted 1984 as its telephone number. Writers of the Budapest Petöfi

Club read *1984* before the 1956 Hungarian uprising, and the BBC's Overseas Service receives reports of the book's continuing popularity in Eastern Europe. Various members of Congress have invoked the image of Big Brother against wiretapping, government personality testing, and plans for a computerized central data bank. The liberal critic Harold Rosenberg said *1984* had set the tone of the postwar imagination by first describing the organization man as "the victim of the dehumanized collective that so haunts our thoughts."

The message that these and many, many others most commonly extract from *1984* lies in its most obviously frightening level: the totalitarian threat to individual freedom from collectives of the right or left. Any book that becomes such common intellectual currency risks being turned into debased coinage, especially when minted by such a critical and nonsystematic intelligence as Orwell's. But equally, any book that can strike such a responsive chord among such natural enemies must say something about the world in which they all live.

What the Orwell cultists cannot take in is his description of the most pervasive development of postwar political thought: the bankruptcy of liberal rationalism. Most of us have been raised on the comforting meliorist belief that if only the weight of human institutions is more equitably distributed, man will at last behave decently and rationally. We may disagree, as

By LAWRENCE MALKIN

33

Mr. Rosenberg, say, disagrees with the John Birch Society, on where the balance of equity lies. But we still believe that ideas can make a more perfect society. Orwell says this simply is not true, or at the very best it is not possible. We have been schooled to believe that the best defense against totalitarian invasions of the privacy of the human spirit must be centered around rationally perfectible institutions. Orwell maintains they are no defense. He warns that the rationalist spirit of progress represents in fact the first step toward the very thing it aims to prevent, because it means giving me the power to enforce my ideas on you.

According to Orwell's timetable, by 1984 institutions of social and political control will have been invented that could, if those guiding them only desired it, solve the problems of mankind by issuing a few orders of the day. But those in power simply refuse to do so. "Sensible men have no power," Orwell said in dismissing the dream of a well-ordered world government. "The energy that actually shapes the world springs from emotions—racial pride, leader-worship, religious belief, love of war—which liberal intellectuals mechanically write off as anachronisms, and which they have usually destroyed so completely in themselves as to have lost all power of action." Orwell wrote those lines in 1941 in an attack on the utopianism of H. G. Wells. Had he lived into another generation, and watched the rise and sometimes tragic fall of American political dynasties with their attendant courts of pundits and professors, I doubt that he would have concluded the sentence as he did. No one could accuse the Kennedy Mafia or Johnson's Texans of forgetting race, leadership, religion, or war. Their overriding concern, however, was the pursuit of political power for its own sake, a pursuit followed at the cost of their sense and their sensibilities. Orwell's most important discovery was that the managers of our society, far from being sensible men, share the irrational

drives of their fellows, and these include power. This is really what frightens us as we watch the liberal imagination turn into a totalitarian nightmare.

As a novel, *1984* is not particularly good. It is more fable than fiction and more fantasy than both. Big Brother is the only character anyone seems to remember, and he probably doesn't even exist. This is quite proper. Big Brother is the symbol and apex of an all-embracing and self-perpetuating state machine called the Party. It is split into an Inner Party (the decision makers) and an Outer Party (middle management). The mass of citizens, called the proles, simply do not count at all in the political scheme. Their lives are dominated by work and poverty, but their emotions are still free.

The plot of *1984* concentrates on the life of Winston Smith, a member of the Outer Party who cannot bear his job of rewriting the past to conform to the Party's directives and simply wants to be left alone. This desire for privacy is, of course, a crime; in every Party member's home stands a two-way telescreen to regulate his behavior and his thoughts. Winston is the last in a consistent line of Orwell's anti-heroes starting with Flory in his novel *Burmese Days*, who said, "Be as degenerate as you can. It all postpones Utopia." Winston's degeneracy consists first in keeping a diary of his private thoughts, then in having a love affair. In *1984* hate is the common emotion; the Two Minutes Hate against the Party's enemies, real or imagined, is a daily ritual. Nevertheless, Julia, a dissident member of the Junior Anti-Sex League, makes clandestine contact with Winston, and they fall in love. All this is watched by the Thought Police. The guilty couple are tricked into a mock conspiracy against the state by O'Brien, a member of the Inner Party and a supremely rational ideologist. He finally tortures Winston into betraying Julia, and at the book's end, into loving Big Brother instead.

Winston's pitiful retreat into privacy, his blowzy love affair, his melodramatic detection, torture, and ex-

tinction as even a pallid individual by the apparatus of the Party, are unworthy of second-rate science fiction. Yet here we are more than halfway to 1984, and the book is still selling in the tens of thousands each year. To find a literary parallel, one would have to reach back beyond the nineteenth-century English novel with its romantic conception of man as a problem solver and into the eighteenth century, where life is larger than man and the world is a wicked place. Winston is a descendant of that almost faceless traveler in strange lands, Lemuel Gulliver.

The book tells us more, much more, about the quality of modern life than about the people in it. Orwell's style, a mixture of ideological fantasy and grubby realism, grows naturally from his beliefs. He confronts ideas with the rough edge of fact. He once wrote of Shakespeare: "he loved the surface of the earth and the process of life," and he could have been writing about himself. By 1984 life has been streamlined to a drab uniformity and the surface of the earth has been paved over, although not without cracks. People have been turned into mere ciphers in a topsy-turvy equation of ideas. The state is organized for war, but War is Peace. A fantastic communications system has been developed (even a "speakwrite" machine), but the Party uses it only to disseminate its own ideas, so Ignorance is Strength. Society has been organized into an immutable hierarchy that frees the individual from even considering his position in it, so Freedom is Slavery. These are the slogans of Oceania. People live by them with an unthinking drudgery. The plastic food has stirring names ("Victory Coffee"). Clothing has no style. Houses are collapsing, and people are crowded into them. Most important, the past is being systematically expunged as part of a process of controlling thought; without human experience, ideas thus can exist in a vacuum. Privacy, individuality, history, tragedy, have vanished. As Winston realizes:

The terrible thing that the Party had done

was to persuade you that mere impulses, mere feelings, were of no account, while at the same time robbing you of all power over the material world. When once you were in the grip of the Party, what you felt or did not feel, what you did or refrained from doing, made literally no difference. Whatever happened you vanished, and neither you nor your actions were ever heard of again. You were lifted clean out of the stream of history. And yet to the people of only two generations ago, this would not have seemed all-important, because they were not attempting to alter history. They were governed by private loyalties which they did not question. What mattered were individual relationships, and a completely helpless gesture, an embrace, a tear, a word spoken to a dying man, could have value in itself. The proles, it suddenly occurred to him, had remained in this condition. . . . they were loyal to one another. . . . The proles had stayed human.

This is not a very helpful view of society for those trying to order it to some predetermined outline. It has never been fashionable for the modern intelligence to consider such human qualities as important *by themselves*. For Orwell, they were the main reason for living. For modern social engineering, human feelings represent unfortunate variables that somehow must be fitted into projections of gross national product (which sound increasingly like those phony figures of rising standards of living blared over the loudspeakers in *1984*); conditioned politically and psychologically for ideological wars in some obscure corner of the world (in *1984* the telescreen carries gruesome pictures of carnage from Malabar—is it?—and announcements of victories that never bring peace any nearer); adjusted willy-nilly for the huge structures of human beings organized to produce, to dwell, and to play together (and you better like it and look the part, for by 1984 you may be guilty of an offense known as "facecrime").

Orwell deliberately ignored the two major areas of the social sciences where the twentieth century has made its strongest advances (if that is what they are): economics and psychology. "Eco-nomic injustice will stop the moment we want it to stop, and no sooner," he wrote in *The Road to Wigan Pier*, "and if we genuinely want it to stop the method adopted hardly matters." Richard Rees, a friend and colleague for twenty years, never once heard Orwell mention Freud, Jung, Kafka, or Dostoevsky. He was not a modern man, and he abhorred systematic (which is not to say critical) thought. By his own admission, he liked gardening, cheese, and even English food. He liked the combination of stolidity and irreverence that marks the English working class, although he never felt at home with them. He was half Eric Blair of Eton and the Imperial Burmese Police, and half down-and-out tramp revolutionary-socialist, a literary propagandist and apocalyptic allegorist who became known as George Orwell. His friends addressed him by the name under which they had first known him; he always meant to change his name legally but never got around to it. In the same way he never really decided who he was, although there was no doubt that his loyalties lay on the left. This constant confrontation of values, shaped by a personal honesty that is unique in modern letters, made Orwell what he was. In a way the nagging dilemma came to a head during the war, when the pacifist and intellectual left revolted him and the rest of England got out and fought. He wrote in 1943: "As to the real moral of the last three years—that the Right has more guts and ability than the Left—no one will face up to it." Indeed, an uncomfortable man to know.

Because *1984* appeared when the postwar Labor government was on its last legs, and because the society it describes lives under a system of government called Ingsoc, the book is often interpreted as the pained protest of a disillusioned socialist. Admittedly, the postwar world of London, with rationing, shortages, and the endless exhortations of the first ideological government England had ever known, provided much color for the book. But Orwell was a far more complex man than that. "I am not a real novelist," Orwell once wrote his friend Julian Symons. "One difficulty I have never solved is that one has masses of experience which one passionately wants to write about . . . and no way of using them up except by disguising them as a novel."

Orwell got the idea for *1984* while working on wartime propaganda for the BBC. He was appalled by the entanglement, perversion, and eventual swallowing up of ideas in the BBC bureaucracy and described the place as "a mixture of a whoreshop and a lunatic asylum." He resigned in 1943 to recover his freedom as a political commentator; just before quitting he wrote a friend: "At present I'm just an orange that's been trodden on by a very dirty boot." (O'Brien says in *1984*: "If you want a picture of the future, imagine a boot stamping on a human face—forever.") The BBC canteen, windowless and underground, was a model for the *1984* cafeteria in the Ministry of Truth (i.e., the propaganda ministry). A wartime colleague tells me that while Orwell survived the stale fish and cabbage smells with less grumbling than most, his imagination dwelt on what the BBC would be like if it were run by a Stalin instead of the liberal muddlers of Broadcasting House.

Orwell was dying of tuberculosis when he wrote the book; the disease killed him in January, 1950, seven months after *1984* was published. It was reviewed on the BBC by Malcolm Muggeridge and Tosco Fyvel, two friends and sometime literary colleagues. Discussing the climactic scene in which Winston breaks down and betrays Julia under threat of having his face chewed by rats, they compared it to the worst imaginings of a pair of prep-school boys trying to scare each other after lights out. Orwell was listening in his hospital bed and laughed out loud. But Orwell refused to accept the thesis of another friend, Arthur Koestler, that political reformism springs from infantile neurosis. His strength lies in his insistence that politics rests on a moral foundation outside the individual and that truth rests in experience outside any system the individual can construct. An individual's search for truth in political life is not purely a function of intellect but of something with an old-fashioned name. The English call it character.

It is no accident that after a lifetime as a political essayist and a writer of starkly realistic novels, Orwell suddenly shifted to allegory in *Animal Farm* and *1984*. It is the literary form best suited to pointing up the contradictions between idea and reality. For Orwell it became the vehicle for explaining the major intellectual event of the first half of this century, the failed utopia—in Russia and elsewhere. The raw material consists of the curiously dated sectarian quarrels of the left in the 1930's, which Orwell freezes forever in the brilliant amber of *Homage to Catalonia*. But the issue described there is still real: freedom vs. power. In a time of social change, how much freedom can be allowed the individual to adjust to it, and at what rate must he adjust? His own or theirs? Totalitarianism insists on controlling the speed of change without reference to individual needs and finally must insist on trying to mold those very needs to fit its predetermined utopia.

Winston, in his subversive notebook, casts utopia aside and insists on following the instincts of his senses—"stones are hard, water is wet"—and finally: "Freedom is the freedom to say that two plus two make four. If that is granted, all else follows." But the catch phrase becomes perverted into the symbol of his humiliating subservience to the Party beyond the bounds of common sense. O'Brien forces him to admit that if the Party decrees it, "two plus two make five." This innumerate slogan has a revealing genesis. In *Assignment in Utopia*, which Orwell read soon after its publication in 1937, at the height of the Soviet purge trials, Eugene Lyons reports that

electric signs were affixed to Moscow buildings with the slogan "$2 + 2 = 5$," exhorting the populace to work hard and complete the then current five-year plan in four years.

"The real answer," Orwell once wrote, "is to dissociate Socialism from Utopianism." The myth of utopia lies as deep in Western culture as that of the Garden of Eden, but it did not come alive politically until Thomas More added topical realism to it in the sixteenth century. As an early humanist, More raised the question of whether utopia could be transferred from the next world to this. As a Christian, he realized that after the Fall and before salvation the answer would have to be no. A utopia of happiness and boredom was literally no place, because of the nature of man and his exposure to the Christian experience—but by 1984 rational idealism has eradicated experience. All ideologies are to some degree utopian, from Pauline Christianity to Bolshevism to the Great Society. To the extent that they are rational and programmatic—and they cannot escape that any more than water can escape being wet—they are subject to disillusion and to perversion by power for its own sake. When More's *Utopia* is translated from the original Latin into modern English, it contains more than a hint of *1984*. Here is a random passage: "wherever you are, you always have to work. There's never any excuse for idleness. There are also no wine-taverns, no ale-houses, no brothels, no opportunities for seduction, no secret meeting-places. Everyone has his eye on you, so you're practically forced to get on with your job, and make some proper use of your spare time." More finally concludes: "Pride would refuse to set foot in paradise, if she thought there'd be no under-privileged classes there to gloat over . . ."

More was a humanist trying to preserve Christian values, Orwell a socialist trying to preserve libertarian values. Later utopians, especially those late Victorians bemused by the deceptively liberating potentialities of technology,

were not so wise. They failed to realize that human experience and philosophical perfection are incompatible. Orwell did, and he turned utopia into "dystopia." Like that other eccentric and pseudonymous English allegorist of modern life, Lewis Carroll, he stepped through the looking glass and parodied rational beliefs to their logical conclusions. Technology, especially the new technology of communications and management, becomes a tyrannical instead of a liberating force in *1984*.

The utopia from which Orwell borrowed most closely was Evgeny Zamyatin's *We*. Zamyatin, a Russian novelist, underwent the enlightening experience of being imprisoned by the czar's police in 1906 and by the Bolsheviks in 1922—in the same corridor of the same prison. He seems, however, to have looked all the way back to Bakunin, the father of anarchism. "I do not want to be I, I want to be We," Bakunin said, alluding to the anarchist's sense of community as a defense against centralized state power. Zamyatin foresaw the collapse of even the community into the state. His book was written in 1923 and set in the year 2600. People have numbers instead of names, and "The Benefactor" rules the "United State." The narrator, D-503, is the mathematician-designer of the first spaceship, soon to be launched carrying the message: "Long live the United State. Long live the Numbers. Long live the Benefactor." D-503's only problem in this well-ordered state is that he suffers from the serious mental disease of imagination. Eventually, after committing the crime of falling in love with beautiful young I-330 and joining her in a rebellion against the "reason" of the United State, he is forced to submit to X-ray treatment that removes the brain center responsible for imagination. He then betrays I-330. Afterward, this chastened number writes: "No more delirium, no absurd metaphors, no feelings—only facts. For I am healthy—perfectly, absolutely healthy . . . I am smiling."

In the end D-503 throws in his lot with law and order: "I am certain we shall win. For Reason must prevail."

Orwell first read Zamyatin's book in 1945, when he was already making notes for *1984*. "What Zamyatin seems to be aiming at," Orwell wrote in a review, "is not any particular country but the implied aims of industrial civilization.... It is in effect a study of the Machine, the genie that man has thoughtlessly let out of its bottle and cannot put back again." Aldous Huxley also seems to have borrowed from *We*, for *Brave New World*. Zamyatin's, Huxley's, and Orwell's books all make similar assumptions about a technological utopia—that it has at last become possible, but that it also will be collectivist, elitist, and incompatible with the ideas of freedom.

In none of these dystopias is physical force the effective agent of control. It is, of course, the ultimate threat—as it must be even in a truly democratic state—but not the proximate one. In the first two the citizens are held down largely by a sort of synthetic happiness, a myth of contentment reinforced by material well-being. For this they have exchanged their freedom. By 1984 the citizens of Oceania have not only lost their freedom but have not even gained happiness for it. Those who wish to retrieve their freedom are subjected to humiliation, loss of identity, and in the last resort, pain. "We shall meet in the place where there is no darkness," O'Brien tells Winston, as he tricks him into disclosing himself as a rebel. This promised utopia turns out to be the torture chambers of the windowless Ministry of Love.

In Orwell's dystopia the proximate agent of control is language. The myths of freedom and peace are kept alive by a hollow language that has completely lost its meaning. In Newspeak, Orwell's most brilliant and culturally incisive creation, language, like personality, has been leached of all flavor. It is "objective," without the subtlety or irony that reflects experience. Newspeak is a caricature of C. K.

Ogden's Basic English, in which the inventor hoped to compress the English language into 850 words. Orwell at first became interested in it as a possible corrective to official euphemism and as a cleansing agent at a time when, he said, most political writing consisted of phrases bolted together like a child's erector set. But he later realized its sinister possibilities when the British government bought the world rights. Syme, a compiler of a Newspeak dictionary in *1984* (he is a bit too clever and is eventually vaporized), knows what it is all about. His team is destroying words by the hundreds every day: "Don't you see that the whole aim of Newspeak is to narrow the range of thought? In the end we shall make thoughtcrime literally impossible, because there will be no words in which to express it.... Every year fewer and fewer words, and the range of consciousness always a little smaller." Newspeak accomplishes this, as Orwell explains in an appendix, by divorcing language from thought. Such words as remain express acceptable ideas or condemn unacceptable ones out of hand. Even by 1984 the process has not been completed, but it is well under way. I have before me a recent release of the "Headquarters, U.S. Military Assistance Command, Vietnam" describing activities of the month. It is interesting to note that the enemy often "attacks" but the "Free World" forces never do; they go on "search and destroy" missions. As usual, the demotic variant, ugly as it may be, is more forceful and more accurate; to "zap." I think Orwell, with his dedication to plain speech, would have been pleased by it.

In truth, everything in 1984 is controlled, ordered, managed. But who shall guard the guardians? In 1984, as ever, no one. Although the concept of an Inner Party can be traced back to Plato, Orwell's most immediate source was the American writer James Burnham, and his book *The Managerial Society*. It provided the ideological

stalking horse for *1984* by predicting the rise of a new managerial class that would not be different from one superstate to another. (Milovan Djilas calls it the New Class in the Communist world.) Burnham foresaw the division of the world into power blocs centered around Europe, Asia, and America, another concept Orwell took over. These managers are described in the theoretical center of *1984*, the book-within-a-book that describes the principles of Ingsoc. Naturally it is forbidden, as is any truthful book. It says:

The new aristocracy was made up for the most part of bureaucrats, scientists, technicians, trade-union organizers, publicity experts, sociologists, teachers, journalists, and professional politicians. These people, whose origins lay in the salaried middle class and the upper grades of the working class, had been shaped and brought together by the barren world of monopoly industry and centralized government. As compared with their opposite numbers in past ages, they were less avaricious, less tempted by luxury, hungrier for pure power, and, above all, more conscious of what they were doing and more intent on crushing opposition.

It would be invidious to put names on this rogues' gallery of twentieth-century American types; I should imagine that for any casual student of the daily newspapers no names would be needed. The essence of Orwell's quarrel with Burnham, and he explains it in two detailed essays, is not that Burnham's description is incorrect but that, having worked it out, he has become fascinated by it and has accepted it as inevitable and therefore even desirable. Orwell labels this, with a kind of political prophecy, "realism." Burnham for a time accepted Nazism as a viable social order—until it began to lose. In England Orwell found that the middle-class managers accepted the Soviet regime, but only *after* it became totalitarian: "Burnham, although the English Russophile intelligentsia would repudiate him, is really voicing their secret wish: the wish to destroy the old, equalitarian version of socialism and usher in a hierarchical society where the intellectual can at last get his hands on the whip."

It is not surprising that when success finally came to Orwell, it was far from sweet and did strange things to this critic of the modern world. After his wife died suddenly in 1945, he retired with their adopted child to the barren and primitive Hebrides to write *1984* in surroundings simpler and more stark than the intellectual hothouse of London liberal society. The move helped break his health. He never bothered to conceal his views; quite the contrary, he exaggerated them to the point of personal abrasion. Michael Ayrton,* then a young artist, recalls that whenever Orwell, wrapped in his old raincoat and scarf, appeared in the local pub, the young people would bemoan the arrival of "Gloomy George." But he loved to entertain friends in his flat for a high tea with English jams and pickles, and when he struck pay dirt with *Animal Farm,* he told his publisher: "At last I can take you out to lunch." Before his death this committed socialist was in the process of turning himself into a limited company to escape England's high income-tax rates.

Animal Farm, the anti-Stalinist satire in which Orwell said he had for the first time managed to fuse artistic and political purpose, had "a hell of a time" finding a publisher. Victor Gollancz, the epitome of the left-wing British intellectual between the wars, refused to publish it although Orwell was under contract to him. "We couldn't have published it then," Gollancz told me several years ago. "Those people were fighting for us, and they had just saved our necks at Stalingrad." T. S. Eliot turned it down for Faber, but on the debatable critical ground that Orwell had failed to bring off the satire. Some Nice Nelly at the Ministry of Information or the publisher Jonathan Cape, Orwell wasn't quite sure which, objected to the use of pigs as a symbol for Bolsheviks. Ironically, Frederic Warburg, no less a middle-

*See "Daedalus and I," page 56.

class, Oxford-educated Jewish liberal intellectual than Gollancz, took on *Animal Farm* and became Orwell's publisher and friend. In the United States Orwell's last books encountered initial misunderstanding that has dogged them ever since. Dial Press wrote Orwell that *Animal Farm* would not do for the American market because it is "impossible to sell animal stories in the USA." A year later, after Harcourt, Brace had accepted it, Dial wrote back and said someone had made a horrible mistake.

Going through the original reviews of *1984* seems to justify the complaint of the Trotskyite historian Isaac Deutscher: "The novel has served as a sort of an ideological super-weapon in the cold war." Scores of American newspaper reviews hailed it as a warning of the menace of "creeping Socialism." In the more liberal big-city press there was an almost grudging admission that tyrannies other than left-wing ones might be involved. Saddest of all is the *New Republic*'s review. "The only thing to guard against is taking it too seriously," wrote Robert Hatch, who refused to believe—and this, in the same decade as Hitler's gas chambers —that men could sink to such depths as to be unable to solve their problems by reason. The English reviewers, less hysterical, more thoughtful and questioning, got closer to the book's human values. They may be summed up by V. S. Pritchett's remark: "The heart sinks but the spirit rebels as one reads Mr. Orwell's opening page."

I don't think Orwell was the least surprised by such massive misunderstandings. ("Of course not," Warburg comments. "He regarded the world as a wicked place.") Orwell meant the book to go into the political arena like all his works and was quite prepared for it to take its lumps there. From his hospital bed he fought back as best he could. He wrote a friend: "I am afraid some of the US Republic papers have tried to use *1984* as propaganda against the Labor Party, but I have issued a

sort of démenti which I hope will be printed."

On June 15, 1949, Warburg dictated a memo containing a statement that Orwell approved. It begins by saying that *1984* is a parody; Orwell does not believe that its details will come true in the Western world, but "something like *1984 could* happen." It continues: "This is the direction in which the world is going at the present time, and the trend lies deep in the political, social and economic foundations of the contemporary world situation. Specifically, the danger lies in the structure imposed on Socialist and Liberal capitalist communities by the necessity to prepare for total war with the USSR and the new weapons, of which of course the atomic bomb is the most powerful and the most publicized. But the danger lies also in the acceptance of a totalitarian outlook by intellectuals of all colors. The moral to be drawn from this dangerous nightmare situation is a simple one: *Don't let it happen to you. It depends on you.*" The memo then cites the dangers of superstates and adds: "The superstates will naturally be in opposition to each other or (a novel point) will pretend to be much more in opposition than they in fact are . . . it is obvious that the Anglo-Americans will not take the name of their opponents and will not dramatize themselves on the scene of history as Communists. The name suggested in *1984* is of course Ingsoc, but in practice a wide range of choices is open. In the USA the phrase 'Americanism' or '100 per cent Americanism' is suitable and the qualifying adjective is as totalitarian as anyone can wish."

As a prophet of specific events, Orwell has a less than perfect record, but only those who want to turn him into the original anti-Communist ideologue could complain of that. Orwell had long before written off the Communist experiment as a brutal failure. He was more immediately concerned with preserving deeper individual values. Ingsoc does not rule the English-speaking world, and we have not been smothered by a blanket of collective thought, at least not yet. Even in the Communist world the plants of individualism keep putting up flowers, if only to be tragically lopped off as soon as they bloom. In any society Orwell's message is what carries the relevance: it still "depends on you" whether or not 1984 comes true. I prefer to think of Julia as the precursor of the slogan that helped ignite a generation: "Make love, not war."

It is comforting to feel that more than halfway to 1984 we have no real Big Brother, and in fact the letters B.B. are more commonly understood nowadays to refer to a French movie star. London today is not the shabby metropolis of 1984. It has given birth to a species of pop culture that, although it may be excessively channeled into the pleasures of personal adornment and self-expression, has at last turned its back on the pretentious mock-aristocratic manners of the middle class that Orwell detested.

On a cool and luscious June day I visited No. 27B Canonbury Square; Orwell's fifth-floor wartime walkup there was the model for Winston Smith's "Victory Mansions." Poor Winston would never have recognized it. The neighborhood is festooned with greenery. Trees line the streets. Children play in the square; old folks sun themselves in it. Across the street, in a beautifully proportioned eighteenth-century mansion rented from the Marquis of Northampton, lives the London correspondent of *The New York Times*. The garden, the brickwork, and even the plumbing of Orwell's old house are in excellent order. Around the corner is an outdoor pub, a rarity in London. It is frequented by a mixture of working-class couples and the chic middle class (Orwell avoided the place because it used to be a hangout for Stalinist intellectuals). The whole neighborhood is urban landscape at its best, but of course property values have skyrocketed. I met a delightful London type tending the garden who could have

been the model for the singing prole woman hanging her washing on the line in *1984*. Of course she remembered Mr. Blair, the writer; she used to work as a housekeeper for the woman who eventually became his second wife. Now she was a pensioner, and her chief worry was that the building had just been sold to some faceless property company. She hadn't even been told its name, and she was afraid she would be evicted and housed in some anonymous government redevelopment scheme far from her old neighborhood. So perhaps Big Brother, unseen as always, is not so distant from Orwell's old back yard after all.

It is easy to draw pictures of bogeymen; the caricature is too quickly adopted as imminent reality, and that is what has happened to Orwell's *1984*. I think Orwell underestimated the strength of European culture in resisting the encroachments of the machine age. The shared experiences that the Party would rub out in 1984 are still very much alive. Surely his own country still contains the sanest, kindest, and probably the most civilized people in Europe or possibly anywhere. Their mature self-awareness expresses itself in an articulate culture that exalts the individual and tolerates his eccentricities. Despite the erosions of two world wars, they cling to a hierarchic social order that encourages self-development, but only within boundaries so comfortably defined that everyone knows the rules of the game stop at actually winning it.

But the threat of 1984 has roosted, like a vulture in a tree, most firmly in the American consciousness. The myths of our competitive culture are coming up against the rough edge of human experience, and the culture itself is shuddering under the strain. The sleek society of managers, the streamlined men whose values lie in sheer accomplishment by control of their environment, has dehumanized itself as Orwell foresaw. Values imposed by work have tended to transcend and sometimes obliterate those that grow

naturally from human contact. The community is a place to *do* something —to work, to play, to sleep—rather than to *be* someone. Synthetic personal contacts through the telescreen ("Good night, David. . . . Good night, Chet.") are more real than everyday life.

The trouble with literary dystopias is that they are essentially negative. Orwell says that "hope lies with the proles"—hope lies with human experience—but it will take a long time. To find a more concrete way out one has to look elsewhere in Orwell's work. It simply will not do to try to turn Orwell into a prophet of anti-Communism or some kind of New Conservative. He simply refuses to get into bed with the left or the right, or any other programmatic apostle. Just before leaving Spain in 1937 he wrote Cyril Connolly: "I have seen wonderful things and at last really believe in Socialism, which I never did before." If his words mean anything, Orwell remained a socialist to his death. But to him socialism was not a programmatic ideology of social and economic change. It dwelt more deeply in the transcendent values of justice, liberty, equality, and the community of feeling (the brotherhood perverted into Big Brother) in which material values play their role alongside human ones. Its primary motives are surely neither rational nor public. Life is held together by family, community, and the shared values and experiences that constitute culture. For the rest of his life Orwell stressed the human and individual quality of this type of socialism. His critics find him gloomy because he returned to classical stoicism and abandoned progress. But without the relativism of ideology to organize human affairs, only the stark absolutes of human character remain. What Orwell is saying is that, now or in 1984, they are the things that really matter.

Lawrence Malkin, a member of the Washington bureau of Time *magazine, spent seven years in London reporting on economic affairs for the Associated Press.*

The Enlightenment

This is our tradition, our world view—the liberal,
rational, humanitarian way of thought
that has persisted for several centuries. This is
the tradition against which
the young rebel. Is it no longer "relevant"?

By PETER GAY

The proposition that the Enlightenment has anything of interest to say to our time sounds at first merely absurd. It sounds like special pleading, the effort of a cloistered scholar to establish some sort of relevance to our impatient time. The Enlightenment seems unreal, a vanished world, charming in the worst possible sense of the word, "historic," wholly remote from us and our pressing needs, as though it were five centuries away, or ten, rather than merely two. We know— are we not often told?—that the age of the Enlightenment was addicted to reason, to optimism, to humanitarianism, to secularism, to rising expectations, and that its self-appointed spokesmen, the philosophes, were a collection of irresponsible literary men, like Voltaire,

or unworldly professors, like Kant, or shallow politician-philosophers, like Jefferson, all guilty of first arousing and then encouraging unjustified expectations.

If this portrait were accurate, the age of the Enlightenment would be nothing more than a condition to which it would be pointless to aspire. And the reforming program of the philosophes would be nothing better than a fantasy that once aroused false hopes, and as its inescapable consequence, produced real despair. At best the Enlightenment would be irrelevant; at worst, it would be pernicious.

But the portrait is, in fact, badly distorted. Each of its lines must be redrawn and assigned new significance. And it is important to undertake this

corrective activity. Santayana once said that those who do not learn from the past will be condemned to repeat it. I may add that those who do not understand the past will be unable to learn from it.

"Enlightenment" is the name given to two distinct but interdependent entities. It is the name of an age, the eighteenth century all across Europe and the European colonies in the New World, and at the same time, the name of a movement that pervaded and came to dominate that age: a movement of philosophes. The two Enlightenments were not the same; Kant, with his customary acuteness, called his age an age of enlightenment, but not an enlightened age; there was, in other words, a great deal of work for

reforming, critical philosophes to do.

It is always perilous to characterize a century with a single epithet, but, taking the risk, I will call the age of the Enlightenment an age of hope. The hope that radiated from scientists and philosophers captured the imagination of a wide public. More and more men came to feel a sense of power over their environment and over their individual destinies. This hope sprang from a number of sources, and it was this confluence of elements that made it so irresistible. And it *was* irresistible. Not merely professional optimists like Condorcet, but hardened realists and unsparing critics of optimism like John Adams, found their age a time that offered solid grounds for self-confidence. Science and its companion, technology,

were opening new, exhilarating vistas into a life that might be longer, easier, pleasanter, safer, than life had ever been before. Science, too, with its spectacular successes, suggested a dependable method for acquiring knowledge outside the increasingly specialized realms of physics or astronomy. Few philosophes were presumptuous enough to deny their forebears all capacity for fruitful thinking, but the scientific thinking of their own day struck them as being a new instrument, far more powerful, far more accurate, than any intellectual instrument ever devised. Scientific thinking was unprecedented and unique in commanding the unanimous assent of informed minds. As the French physiocrats put it, a little quaintly, Euclid had been

A contemporary view of The Philosophes at Supper *was engraved by the Swiss artist Jean Huber, who specialized in caricatures of Voltaire (1), shown above as a wizened little man with his arm raised. Also seated around the table, and identified by numerals, are the following philosophes: (2) Le Père Adam, a Jesuit priest who became Voltaire's secretary; (3) Abbé Jean Maury, skeptical cleric and friend of Diderot's; (4) Jean d'Alembert, famed mathematician and co-editor with Diderot of the* Encyclopédie; *(5) the Marquis de Condorcet, radical political philosopher and later a victim of the Jacobin Reign of Terror; (6) Denis Diderot, editor of the Enlightenment's compendium of rational knowledge, the* Encyclopédie; *and (7) Jean de La Harpe, dramatist, critic, and protégé of Voltaire's. The figures standing around the table have no counterparts in real life.*

Voltaire
(1694–1778)

Among the men of the Enlightenment François Marie Arouet, self-styled Voltaire, stands first. The acid skepticism, the faith in nature and science, the hatred of theologians and dogmamongers, all this had already been formulated when Voltaire was still a fashionable young playwright making his way into aristocratic salons. What Voltaire did was to say it more crisply, more often, with more sheer wit and aplomb than anyone had said it before: he made "enlightenment" the common attitude of the educated men of his day.

Before Voltaire deism had been the "rational religion" of a few rarefied souls. Voltaire made it seem the quintessence of reason and goodness. Regarding the deeper mysteries of faith, Voltaire had his ready answer: Do not fret about the unknowable. Let us keep busy and useful and "cultivate our garden."

His failings were many. He exposed superstitions but thought them good enough for the "rabble." He fought injustice but defended absolute monarchy. In the end such failings hardly mattered. In 1791, when the revolutionary National Assembly ordered his long-dead remains transferred to the Paris Pantheon, scores of thousands followed the bier, which bore the inscription by which men chose to remember him: "He taught us to be free."

the greatest despot who ever lived—his propositions had compelled the agreement of all men of intelligence and goodwill. Philosophy, the philosophes argued, ought to imitate the exact sciences and produce ideas that could be corrected, refined, and improved upon, so that they could be universally accepted as no philosophical system or theological doctrine had ever been or could ever be accepted.

This quality of the enlightened mind deserves emphasis, for it separates the eighteenth century from its predecessors and places it into direct relation with our own. Voltaire saw history aspiring to the condition of a science; Adam Smith dismissed the "political arithmetic" of earlier economists as inadequately precise; the authors of the Federalist papers spoke proudly of the advances that the "science of politics" had made in their own time. It is characteristic of the age of the Enlightenment that the sciences of man—psychology, political economy, political science, cultural history, sociology—should take their beginning then. And the leading practitioners of these new sciences—nearly all of them philosophes—steadily reiterated that they had two related purposes: to establish objective, general truths about man and his conduct, and to establish these truths principally for the sake of improving man's lot.

The pervasive hope that animated the eighteenth century did not emerge from intellectual inventions alone. All around them men saw evidence of improvement, most of all in medicine. Eighteenth-century medicine looks unimpressive to us, even deadly; but its contemporaries found it enormously promising. We are more skeptical in assigning causal importance to a single element; we are inclined to doubt that the disappearance of pestilence and the reduction of famines, like the palpable increase in population all across Europe, were somehow the work of improved medical attention. But the eighteenth century found the scanty

statistics spectacular and gratifying: they took the growth of population as a good sign, as a sign of rising hopes for all. The pessimism of Thomas Malthus came at the end—in many ways it *marked* the end—of the age of the Enlightenment.

This was not all. The conduct of all classes—even the upper classes—seemed to be improving. There was more talk and less violence; reforming causes like the antislavery crusade were receiving a serious hearing. Horace Walpole—no optimist—thought it a splendid century. Reason, he wrote, had finally begun to "attain that ascendant in the affairs of the world" that it deserved to attain; while prejudices and tyrannies survived, they had at least produced no new "persecutors or martyrs." It was remarkable, he thought: "No prime ministers perished on a scaffold, no heretics in the flames: a Russian Princess spared her competitor; even in Turkey the bowstring has been relaxed."

These improvements, and many others, were by no means universal. In recent years social historians have insistently reminded us that in the eighteenth century the poor remained as poor as they had always been; that short life expectancies remained the rule among the majority of people; that while epidemics loosened their deadly grip, the lower classes continued to die in uncounted numbers, and while famine officially disappeared, many unofficially still starved to death. Exploitation did not vanish with the new industrial techniques that spread, slowly at first and then more rapidly, through England and across Europe. It merely took new, often more savage, forms. The law, a cherished province of the reforming philosophes, grew more repressive as the possessing classes sought to protect themselves from the most petty thievery by enlarging the list of crimes for which the death penalty could be imposed. Yet, when all these allowances have been made, when we keep in the forefront of our minds that records are normally left by those who are fortunate enough to be literate, it still remains true that the general color of life was brighter and that hope grew, like a beneficent weed, unchecked.

It was in direct response to this hope that the philosophes developed their program. If the philosophes were reformers, they were so for two reasons: they had cause to think that their program had a chance of realization, and they continued to have a great deal of work to do. Far from being utopians, the philosophes sensed the mood of their century and sought to capture its public opinion and influence its direction. But it was the direction in which the century was going in any event, if a little more slowly than the impatient philosophes hoped it would. In a word, for the eighteenth century optimism was realism, or to put it another way: the philosophy of the Enlightenment was the philosophy that the age of the Enlightenment wanted, needed, and deserved.

Thus, just as the philosophes' optimism was more reasonable than many have long believed, so was it more moderate. Nothing would be easier (nothing, in the light of the textbooks, seems more necessary) than to compile a little library of pessimistic pronouncements by philosophes of all countries, by Germans like Wieland and Scots like Hume, by Frenchmen like Voltaire and Italians like Beccaria. All these philosophes were men of good hope, but none trusted themselves to a theory of progress. All thought well of the prospects of human reason, but none ever said, or ever believed, that it would triumph totally or for all time.

Indeed, the Enlightenment's view of reason itself was a complicated, highly nuanced affair. Far from denigrating passion, the philosophes appreciated its power and valued its work. They persistently assailed Christianity—it was their main enemy—because Christianity seemed to them the deadly adversary not merely of reason but of passion as well. Everyone recalls David

Hume's remark that "reason is, and ought to be, the slave of the passions," but few have treated that remark with the seriousness it demands. With a vigor that some modern playwrights would appreciate, the philosophes honored the claims of the body and celebrated the pleasures of sensuality—within reason, no doubt, but vigorously nonetheless. Nor is this all. The Enlightenment's admiration for reason was, to use modern language, confidence in the scientific method. The philosophes' unceasing complaints against the seventeenth-century metaphysicians and their ambitious rationalist systems—coupled with their equally unceasing advocacy of Newton's "philosophical modesty"—make the men of the Enlightenment into apostles of experience, into pragmatists who insisted on testing each proposition or each institution by its works rather than by its façade.

Thus corrected, the Enlightenment appears rather more complicated and much more reasonable than before. It becomes possible to see the Enlightenment not as a fossil, to be displayed in a glass case for our distant admiration or yawning indifference, but as a force, to be used.

But how? Let us grant that the leading historians of the Enlightenment—Hume and Voltaire, Robertson and Gibbon—were the first modern historians; still their moralizing and their preoccupation with the failings of Christianity compromise the value of their histories as working models for historians of our own day. Let us grant that the leading sociologists of the Enlightenment—Montesquieu and Hume, Ferguson and Adam Smith—were the first modern sociologists; still their inadequate data and primitive theories reduce their books, fascinating as they may be, to distant ancestors of the sociology books we study today. Let us grant that the aestheticians of the Enlightenment—Dubos and Hume, Diderot and Kant—were the first modern aestheticians; still their bid for aesthetic

Gotthold Lessing
(1729–1781)

It says much about the Enlightenment spirit that the playwright Gotthold Lessing preferred to look upon himself as a critic. It says much about Lessing the critic that his greatest work of poetic criticism was entitled *Laokoon*. To Lessing, the critic's heroic role was to destroy the serpent of superstition, conformity, and pedantry that strangles man's reason, his feelings, his sentiments, and his imagination. It was Lessing who championed Shakespeare against the rule-bound classical drama of Racine and Voltaire. It was Lessing who championed freethinking against bigoted German theologians and then championed the "inner truths" of religion against the freethinking deists themselves.

In his life and in his work he was distinguished by a manly openness of spirit. It was characteristic of Lessing that his most famous play, *Nathan the Wise*, was meant to demonstrate that nobility of spirit can be associated with any religious creed. It typified that same open spirit that Lessing saw the history of all religions as a record of man's continuing "education" in knowledge of the Divine. When Lessing died, famous and nearly penniless, it was Goethe who paid pregnant tribute to his brave and generous spirit: "We have lost," said Goethe, "more than we think."

David Hume
(1711–1776)

When Hume came to Paris in 1763, the philosophes, enlightened noblemen, and fashionable hostesses all rushed to acclaim him. From his estate in Ferney, Voltaire greeted Hume as "my St. David," while in Paris Mme d'Épinay reported that "no feast is complete without him." Even Mme Pompadour fluttered around the fifty-two-year-old Scottish philosopher whose youthful *Treatise of Human Nature* had borne the subtitle *Being an Attempt to Apply the Experimental Method of Reasoning to Moral Subjects* and whose "Natural History of Religion" had sabotaged revealed religion by quietly treating it as a mere phenomenon.

Yet the Paris philosophes failed to see that they were clutching a dangerous genius to their bosom. For the enlightened philosophy of Hume subverted the Enlightenment. The philosophes believed in scientific law; Hume's analysis demolished the traditional concept of cause and effect. The philosophes believed that God the Creator could be deduced from the Creation; Hume demolished that deist argument as well. The philosophes looked for a morality based on reason; Hume showed that morality derives from the passions. Himself an easygoing worldling, Hume left the structure of human thought far shakier than any philosophe imagined it could be.

freedom was so closely bound up with neoclassicism that their concerns are no longer ours. Perhaps most troubling of all: let us grant that the reformers of the Enlightenment (and that includes practically all the philosophes in all the countries that could boast of an Enlightenment) were the first modern reformers—they hated slavery, deplored poverty, denounced the cruelty of criminal law and the dead hand of the censor, and decried the subjection of women and children—and that their goals remain recognizable and indeed admirable; yet their specific proposals strike us as halfhearted, tepid, and indeed, irrelevant—irrelevant in part because they have already been achieved, in part because they no longer seem to matter, or to be enough.

If we could restore a philosophe to life and confront him with the distance between his time and ours, he would, I think, welcome rather than deplore that distance as a sign of his, and his movement's, success. After all, the philosophes sought to make knowledge scientific, which, as I have said, is self-corrective and progressive. If they often did not succeed, if they carried a heavier burden of unexamined assumptions and hasty conclusions than they knew, if their very procedures have required marked amendment, reformulation, sophistication, these in themselves do not make the Enlightenment irrelevant. Was it not of the very nature of their thought to invite and welcome change, even in the method of thinking itself?

It is with this question that we have reached the heart of the Enlightenment's thought and the surviving meaning of the Enlightenment for our time—its method. The secularism of the philosophes was at least partly a sectarian quarrel with Christianity. The philosophes paid a price for their bellicosity: being at war, they had no perspective on what they persisted in thinking of as the enemy; they could never fairly assess the contours of Christian thought, Christian art, Chris-

tian humanitarianism—in short, Christian civilization.

But the issue at stake in their monotonous exposures of the wickedness of priests, the presumption of theologians, and the contradictions in Holy Writ was actually of the highest importance. The philosophes sought to extend critical thinking to all areas of human life and belief, to extend it even to—especially to—those sacred precincts that had normally escaped scrutiny: the legitimacy of dominant authorities, the conduct of the ruling house, the logic of the state religion. Gibbon's cynical observations on the religious policies of the Roman emperors and Voltaire's sardonic dissection of the apologetic gymnastics of contemporary theologians may have been deficient in humanity, but they point directly to the Enlightenment's most significant contribution to its time, and if we will only listen, to ours: they are direct assaults on the formidable citadel of untested belief.

Criticism, it is often said, is not enough. One cannot live by method alone. But the criticism of the Enlightenment was more than destructiveness, its method was more than a method. Each implied a philosophy of man. The great critics of more recent years—Marx, Nietzsche, Freud—all in decisive ways children of the Enlightenment, exercised their critical faculties and developed their critical techniques not for some malicious private pleasure. They sought instead to penetrate beyond appearances to realities, to see through the cant of theologians, politicians—and historians—to expose man's unconscious self-deceptions for the sake of greater jurisdiction over events.

But these later critics did their thinking in their own way; they found new terrain on which to stand. This, I must repeat, was only proper. A twentieth-century thinker who sought in all ways to imitate Lessing or Voltaire or Hume would in no way be like them. He would be a slave to books; they were pupils of experience. He would be an antiquary, losing nothing of his models but their spirit. The authentic admirer of the age of the Enlightenment will show his admiration by moving beyond it.

But in what direction? Our time, it seems, in its mood, in its general temper, is the antithesis of the Enlightenment; reasonable though the Enlightenment's self-confidence may have been, our self-doubt seems just as reasonable. Both appear as appropriate responses to experience. I need not rehearse again, at length, the malaise of our age. The threat, or the temptation, of unreason is everywhere. It is not merely that we have discovered the powers of unreason; reason itself seems to have gone mad. The worst creations of our time—the manipulation of the buying public and the violation of privacy by powerful agencies, the brainwashing practiced by the Chinese Communists and the mass murder practiced by the Nazis, the abuse of our environment and the callousness of world politics —are all products of invention, of calculation, of experiment, of practical reason in the service of profit, degradation, and murder. Science, once man's great hope, has become our nightmare.

I do not mean to make light of our terrors, our victims, and our gloomy prospects when I add to this conventional catalogue of horrors a few unfashionable dashes of hope. With all our anguish, beneath the surface of our lives there are, I think, certain elements of soundness. The very weakness of Europe, the very failures of our foreign policy, suggest that amidst turmoil, ugliness, and suffering, a global civilization may be near birth. Just as four hundred years ago the French *Politiques* advanced the novel and utterly subversive notion that men of differing religious persuasions could live together in the same country, under the same sovereign, so we are witnessing the spread of the equally novel and equally subversive idea that all-out war is nonsensical, impractical, impossible. It may be cold comfort indeed in the wasteland of our century, but we are still here; and that, in the face of Nothing, is better than nothing. Similarly, the rebellions of the young and of the blacks in this country, as elsewhere, are rich in ambiguous and unexplored possibilities.

The decisive question, of course, is, what will we do with it all? Will we be victims or guides? And it is here that the Enlightenment continues to have validity for us and may still exercise a significant and beneficent influence on our civilization. For what the Enlightenment did, with its championship of criticism and its insistence on the right of uncompromising examination of everything, was to show man the way to autonomy—that is, to responsible freedom. Autonomy, Kant said, speaking for the Enlightenment in the years of its close, is the freedom to obey rational laws. This dictum looks at first glance a little obscure—what freedom is there in obedience? But in fact the dictum sums up, with splendid economy, the meaning of the Enlightenment's critical method. It holds that to obey every fleeting impulse, to follow every whim, to surrender to every passion, is not freedom but anarchy, which is merely another form of slavery. The free man follows law, but his freedom lies in his knowledge that he himself has freely made that law and that it is legislation that has emerged from his continuous and critical examination of his environment, his possibilities, and himself. Such law gives not merely self-control but control of one's fate to the extent that it lies within man's control. Only by following this method, and by rejecting easy compromises and the strangely seductive charms of despair, can man master the world he has made.

Peter Gay's most recent contribution to HORIZON *was "The Weimar Resemblance," in the Winter, 1970, issue. He is the author of* The Enlightenment, *which won the National Book Award for History when it was published in 1966.*

**Thomas Jefferson
(1743–1826)**

It is not customary to consider Jefferson a figure of the Enlightenment, yet in a sense he was one of its greatest men. This was not because his philosophical views coincided with those of the Paris philosophes, though they did and markedly so. Like Voltaire, Jefferson dabbled in science, and as president of the American Philosophical Society he delivered a learned report on fossil remains. Like most French philosophes—many of whom he met during his diplomatic sojourn in Paris between 1784 and 1789—he distrusted priests, hated "every form of tyranny over the mind of man," looked on Jesus as the "benevolent Moralist" and upon Bacon, Newton, and Locke as "my trinity of the three greatest men the world has ever produced."

What truly made Jefferson a great Enlightenment figure was something else. He was the Enlightenment in action, for he took the Enlightenment's ultimate principle—the faith that men are noblest when they are free—and helped give that principle its necessary political form: the form of a republic constituted for freedom and self-government. In doing so, Jefferson made the Enlightenment more than a passing phase in the history of "ideas." He, more than any other single man, made it a permanent presence among men.

Who Needs Computers

...With Mathematical Prodigies Like These?

By J. BRYAN, III

Cyrus the Great could address every soldier in his army by name. Léon Gambetta, the French statesman, could quote thousands of pages of Victor Hugo verbatim. Mathurin Veysierre of Prussia could listen to twelve different sentences in twelve different languages, all strange to him, and repeat them syllable for syllable. Possessors of these preternaturally powerful memories are called eidetics. They may also be called freaks. Along with clairvoyants, telepaths, and people blessed with perfect pitch, they are the mental equivalents of albinos, dwarfs, and people cursed with color blindness. Nature's hand twitched at the moment she minted each of them.

Eidetics come in several grades, and I have to warn you that Cyrus, Gambetta, and Veysierre, astounding as their feats were, rank very near the bottom. Their memories were mere freezers that kept fresh a name or a page or a sound until it was needed again. Nothing *happened* to the deposit. It did not mature, like wine or a bond; it simply dozed. On the other hand, consider Paul Morphy of New Orleans (b. 1837), who once played eight games of chess simultaneously against eight expert opponents, winning six games, losing one, and tying one. You're not impressed? Let me finish: Morphy was blindfolded. J. H. Blackburne of London once played twelve such games. He had not only to visualize the positions of 384 chessmen but to revise his mental images after every move. More than that, he had at the same time to plan twelve separate campaigns. Passive memory was not enough here; it had to be supplemented by continuous and intense cogitation. If we think of Gambetta's recital as equivalent to the running of a mile in three minutes, surely Morphy and

Blackburne each ran it in two minutes.

There are other eidetics who rank close to the blindfolded chess-players, but whether close ahead or close behind I have never been able to decide. Some of their feats are so difficult as to seem incredible, even impossible. I have in mind the lightning calculators, those mental marvels who can rattle off the answer to a long-drawn-out problem in arithmetic almost before it is stated—and without pencil and paper, of course. For instance, Oscar Verhaege (b. 1862), a Belgian, squared 888,888,888,888,888 in forty seconds; later he raised 9,999,999 to the fifth power in sixty seconds; the answer ran to thirty-five digits. Jacques Inaudi (b. 1867), an Italian, memorized a one-hundred-digit number in twelve minutes; he could tell the day of the week on which a given date falls; and he also had the unique gift of being able to express a number less than 100,000 as the sum of four squares—this when still in his teens. Truman Henry Safford (b. 1836), an American, was asked to square 365,365,365,365,365,365. "In no more than one minute" he gave the answer: 133,491,850,208,566,925,016,-658,299,941,583,225. Safford was then ten years old. Zerah Colburn (b. 1804), also an American, was challenged to raise 8 to the sixteenth power and gave the answer "in a few seconds": 281,-474,976,710,656. Colburn was *eight!*

True, Mozart was composing minuets before he was four; John Stuart Mill was learning Greek at the age of three; William Crotch played "God Save the King" on the organ, treble and bass, at two years and three months, and Christian Heinecken is said to have memorized the principal events in the Pentateuch at twelve months. But are these other *Wunderkinder* more impressive—more *prodi-*

gious, if you wish—than Colburn and Safford?

Very well. We'll suspend judgment until we've looked at more of them. One of the most thoroughly documented calculators was Jedediah Buxton of Derbyshire (b. 1707). Buxton's specialty was interpreting the infinitely large in terms of the infinitesimally small: how many cubic eighths of an inch in a rectangular block of stone 23,145,789 yards long by 5,642,732 wide by 54,965 thick? how many grains of corn (dimensions given) in a bin whose volume is 202,680,000,360 cubic miles? He had never heard of billions and trillions, much less the still higher multiples of 1,000, so he made up his own names for two of them: the cube of 1,000,000 (a quintillion) he called a "tribe"; a tribe of tribes (an undecillion—the figure 1 followed by thirty-six zeroes) was a "cramp."

When Buxton visited London to be examined by the Royal Society, his hosts took him to see Garrick in *Richard III*. The plot meant nothing to him; he focused his whole attention on counting the words each actor spoke and the number of steps each took. Unlike most eidetics, he found a practical application for his gift: he could glance at any field, whatever its shape, and announce a minutely accurate estimate of its acreage. "In this manner he measured the whole lordship of Elmeton and brought [the owner] the contents not only in acres, but even in square inches."

Johann Dase of Hamburg (b. 1824) multiplied two numbers of twenty digits each in six minutes, two of forty in forty minutes, and two of one hundred in eight hours and forty-five minutes. His memory was so tenacious that two hours after his performance he could repeat all the numbers he had

What is 8 raised to the sixteenth power?

used. He shared Buxton's gift of instantaneous estimate; one glance told him the number of letters in a line of type or the pips in a spread of dominoes. (As a child Rex Stout, the creator of Nero Wolfe, gave exhibitions in which he would glance at a column of figures and immediately announce the total.) Dase chose for his masterwork a tabulation of the factors of all the numbers from 7,000,000 to 10,000,000. He had factored about half when he died.

George Parker Bidder of Devonshire (b. 1806) started out along Buxton's line of the infinite/infinitesimal. Asked how many hogsheads of cider could be pressed from 1,000,000 apples if 30 apples make a quart, the ten-year-old boy gave the correct answer in thirty-five seconds: 132 hogsheads, 17 gallons, and 1 quart, with 10 apples over. Two years later he was told that a certain pendulum oscillated $9\frac{3}{4}$ inches per second and asked how far it would travel in 7 years, 14 days, 2 hours, 1 minute, and 56 seconds, allowing 365 days, 5 hours, 48 minutes, and 55 seconds to a year. He gave the answer in less than a minute: $2,165,625,744\frac{3}{4}$ inches. His precocity inevitably attracted smart alecks. One asked him, "How many bull's-tails would it take to reach the moon?" Young Bidder's reply anticipated Lincoln: "One, if it is long enough."

Like Dase's, Bidder's ability soon transcended the mere piling of digit upon digit. He was still only fourteen when he was asked for a number whose cube minus 19, times its cube, equals the cube of 6; his answer, 3, was given "instantly." So was his answer when asked to find two numbers whose difference is 12 and whose product times their sum equals 14,560 (they are 26 and 14). Bidder enjoyed no celebrity in his own family. One of his brothers knew the Bible by heart. Another, an actuary, lost his ledgers in a fire and rewrote them from memory; the task took six months and brought on a fatal attack of brain fever. George Bidder retained his powers until his death. Shortly before it came, a friend happened to remark that if light travels 190,000 miles per second (correctly, 186,300), and if the 36,918 waves of red light needed to create the impression of red occupy only one inch, the total number of waves that strike the eye in one second must be enormous.

"You needn't work it out," Bidder told him. "The number will be four hundred and forty-four trillion, four hundred and thirty-three billion, six hundred and fifty-one million, two hundred thousand." Correct.

I have notes on several other calculators, but before I do more than merely list them—Henri Mondeux (b. 1826), Charles Grandemange (b. 1835), and one Prolongeau (birth date and full name unknown to me), all of France; Thomas Fuller of Virginia (b. about 1710); and Vito Mangiamele of Sicily (b. 1826)—I want to return to an earlier statement: Jacques Inaudi "could tell the day of the week on which a given date falls." This may be the most mysterious of Nature's freakish gifts. Compared with it, Buxton's ability to estimate acreage at a glance seems child's play. How is it *possible* for someone to tell you *instantly* that August 28, 1591, was a Wednesday? Yet there are persons who can do it, persons alive today; for instance, the twin brothers Charles and George (last name suppressed), who are subjects of a continuing study at the New York State Psychiatric Institute. Ask them when Easter will fall in 1982, and their answer comes almost simultaneously with the end of your question. Here is a fragment of dialogue between the twins and an examiner:

"In what months of the year 2002 does the first of the month fall on a Friday?"

"February, March, and November."

"When did April twenty-first lately fall on a Sunday?"

"In 1968, 1963, 1957, 1946 . . ."

And then this: "What is seven times four?"

"Two."

The psychiatric term for Charles and George is "idiot savants." Although they are thirty years old, their mental age is between eight and ten. They are, as you have seen, quite unable to do basic arithmetic; yet in addition to having a permanent calendar at their tonguetips, they can gabble an exhaustive account of everything that happened to them on any day of their post-infancy lives. The weather is always prominent in these accounts. Examiners check the official weather reports for the day chosen, and they have never caught the twins in an error.

I think we now have enough cases to warrant an inquiry of whether any pattern is discernible among our eidetics. Well, Oscar Verhaege, the boy who squared 888,888,888,888,888 in forty seconds, was another idiot savant; at seventeen he still "expressed himself like a two-year-old baby." Mondeux, Mangiamele, and Inaudi were shepherds; counting sheep seems to have sharpened them, instead of putting them to sleep. Buxton, a farm hand, and Fuller, a Negro slave, were illiterates. Mondeux and Safford were unbalanced; listen to a description of Safford in mid-calculation: "He flew around the room like a top, pulled his pantaloons over the top of his boots, bit his hands, rolled his eyes in their sockets, sometimes smiling and talking, and then seeming to be in an agony. . . ." Blackburne, the blindfolded chess-player, was "liable to get very violent at times," and Morphy died insane. Colburn had an extra finger on each hand, whereas—here is an odd congruity for you!—both Grandemange and Prolongeau were born without arms and legs.

In short, of all these brilliant men, George Bidder alone was normal. Yet even he shared one common denominator with the rest. Have you noticed it? They are all men. There is not a woman among them.

Passed to the Lucy Stone League for comment.

J. Bryan admits that the "III" after his name represents almost the longest number he is capable of remembering without the assistance of pencil and shirt cuff.

A handsome, intense young actor, Artaud portrays a monk in the film La Passion de Jeanne d'Arc *in 1928.*

Ravaged, old at the age of fifty-two, a tortured Artaud speaks to an interviewer in 1948, the year of his death.

A VOCATION FOR MADNESS

"Sickness is a state," wrote Artaud, "and health is but another state, worse, more cowardly, and more mediocre"

Antonin Artaud was born in Marseille on September 4, 1896, the son of a well-to-do shipowner and his Greek-born wife. In later life, having regressed to what Freud called the pregenital stage, Artaud's horror of sexuality led him to deny that he had been born of woman. He wrote a friend: "I was born at 4 rue du Jardin des Plantes [so far so good] from a uterus where I had no need to be and which I never needed, for that is no way to be born, copulated and massaged nine months by a membrane, the yawning membrane that devours without teeth, as the Upanishads say, and I knew that I was born otherwise, of my works and not of a mother."

Artaud also sometimes claimed that he was the child of a man and a succubus, a female demon. In fact, the pain of his early years came not from a strange birth but from his mother's loss of two children in infancy and from his own poor health—he caught meningitis at the age of five and almost lost his life. The Artaud household was visited by doctors who came not to heal but to announce the deaths of his infant brother and sister. The doctors told Artaud's mother to mix his evil-tasting medicines with jam to make them palatable. He was to maintain the belief that what is enticing is also poisonous.

Warmth and affection he associated less with his parents than with the Greek grandmother he visited in Smyrna, who coddled the frail, high-strung child and gave him the pet name Nanaqui. Years later, from the depths of the insane asylum to which he had been committed, Artaud began to sign his letters to friends as Nanaqui. He had learned at an early age that the world is dangerous, that life is easily lost, and that protection must be sought, if only in the comforting sound of a pet name.

He was constantly ill, afflicted with nervous disorders, facial tics, and stuttering. Illness was a way of claiming his mother's attention. Throughout his life he was to plead for special consideration on the grounds that he was suffering, and different from other men. Artaud the writer should be allowed to publish and Artaud the actor to act, not only because of the merit of his work, but because it was the work of a man physiologically and psychologically stricken. "I used my mental illness like an emblem, like a flag," he wrote the editor of the *Nouvelle Revue Française*, Jean Paulhan. He believed that illness gave an extra dimension to his acting. When he learned that the director Abel Gance was filming *The Fall of the House of Usher*, he wrote to him: "I do not propose myself for the part, I demand it. John Barrymore could do it magnificently from the out-side, whereas I would do it from the in-side. My life is the life of Usher in his sinister house. I have pestilence in my soul. There is a quality of nervous suffering that the greatest actor in the world can only re-create in a film if he has experienced it."

Artaud's illness also allowed him to escape the family tradition that the eldest son must enter the shipping business. When he was fourteen, he founded a poetry magazine. Five years later he was committed to a rest home after tearing up everything he had written and giving away his personal belongings to friends. World War I saw him briefly in uniform, but he was discharged at the end of nine months for sleepwalking. From 1918 to 1920 he was in and out of rest homes in France and Switzerland, and it was at this time that he started taking drugs, which he was to do more or less constantly for the rest of his life. Again he used his illness as an explanation, saying that addicts feel more strongly than others what is missing in life.

Like any provincial French youth with artistic inclinations, he wanted to rise to Paris (*monter à Paris*, as the French say), and arrangements were made with a well-known psychiatrist, Doctor Toulouse, for Artaud to board at his hospital in the Paris suburb of Villejuif. When Artaud arrived in 1920, Doctor Toulouse accepted him as a

By SANCHE DE GRAMONT

member of his family, because, the doctor said, "I understood at once that I had never before met such an exceptional person, of the race of Baudelaire, Nerval, and Nietzsche." Photographs of this period show Artaud looking like an archangel, fiery but pure, with silky, luxuriant hair, a direct, candid gaze, and an expression of gentle resolution on his face. Later photographs of Artaud remind one of a stretch of perfect coastline that has been struck by a tornado.

But for more than fifteen years Artaud functioned in Paris in spite of, or perhaps because of, his illness. He was amazingly prolific. He acted on the stage and in films, he wrote articles and books, he founded a repertory company, and he published the theatrical theories that have become so influential. After this long productive period, and through a set of circumstances that will be examined later, Artaud was committed to an asylum for the insane and remained in confinement for nine years.

Two French doctors who have written about Artaud see him as a classic illustration of schizophrenia—the inability to build his own world with others, the conviction that demons had taken hold of him, and the fear of sexuality, which he associated with disease and microbes. They see the symptoms of schizophrenia in Artaud's belief that he was made of glass and was breakable, in his vertigo, in his fear of noises, in his often incomprehensible language, and in his identification with the dead (he wrote an article in which he identified himself with the Renaissance painter Paolo Uccello). He also suffered acute physical pain, migraine, temporary paralysis, and lack of coordination. At the end of his life he habitually jabbed his head with the point of a knife, as though he were performing an instinctive form of acupuncture.

The two doctors interpret Artaud's creative achievements as a form of therapy, as an activity that brought relief from his mental illness and allowed him, at the same time, to keep a grip on reality.

But Artaud never wanted to be cured. If he was mad, he welcomed his madness. He did not hope that writing and acting would help make him well. On the contrary, he felt that it was only because he was ill that he was able to create and that his illness gave his work a special quality. Much of his writing was an inquiry into the limits and definition of his madness. "Sickness is a state," he wrote, "and health is but another state, worse, more cowardly, and more mediocre." To him the rational world was deficient; he welcomed the hallucinations that abolished reason and gave meaning to his alienation. He purposely placed himself outside the limits in which sanity and madness can be opposed, and gave himself up to a private world of magic and irrational visions. As one of his friends said, "he had a vocation for madness, he entered it as one enters the priesthood." Artaud could have served as a model for psychoanalysts like Georg Groddeck, a contemporary of Freud and author of *The Book of the It*, who believed that illness was a vital expression of the human organism, and that every illness, mental or physical, was caused by an inner conflict.

"I do maintain that man creates his own illness for a definite purpose," wrote Groddeck, "using the outer world merely as an instrument, finding there an inexhaustible supply of material which he can use for this purpose, today a piece of orange peel, tomorrow the spirochete of syphilis, the day after a draft of cold air, or anything else that will help him pile up his woes."

The artist, in Groddeck's view, is by definition a patient, but one who is able to exploit his sickness: "The artist is not an interesting cripple but someone who has by the surrender of his ego to the flux of the It (the mysterious power which animates man) become the agent and translator of the extra-causal forces which rule us." Artaud would have approved without qualifi-

cation. He often said that he was "exploiting his madness."

Three years after his arrival in Paris Artaud sent some poems to the *Nouvelle Revue Française*, then the most respected literary magazine in France. The editor, Jacques Rivière, rejected the poetry but was interested enough to want to meet the poet. After their first meeting Artaud wrote Rivière to explain that his poetry should not be judged by ordinary standards because he was radically, physiologically, different and could not adapt his literary style to the editorial requirements of this or that publication. What seemed to Rivière to be literary defects were, Artaud said, but the symptoms of "a fearful mental disease. My ideas abandon me at every stage . . . I live beneath myself, and I suffer from it, but I accept it for fear of dying completely . . . The few things I sent you are fragments I was able to rescue from complete nothingness." Rivière was sympathetic and encouraged Artaud to try to control his images better; he clearly had not understood what was involved. Artaud insisted in another letter that any "defects of form . . . are not to be attributed to a lack of practice or mastery . . . but to a collapse of the soul at its center, a kind of erosion of ideas . . . there is something that destroys my thinking, something that prevents me from being what I could be, but that leaves me, as it were, in suspense."

Rivière replied with bromides—try not to think about it; others are in your condition. But at least Artaud had succeeded in being treated by him, not as an aspiring writer, but as a man in distress to whom publication was a form of rescue. Although he never really grasped that Artaud could not control what he wrote, Rivière did recognize the *cri de coeur* in his letters and offered to publish their correspondence. Again it was thanks to his illness that Artaud attained recognition in the pages of the highly orthodox *Nouvelle Revue Française*.

Artaud had not come to Paris to be

a writer, however, but to be an actor. He was hired by Charles Dullin, whose Théâtre de l'Atelier was the most interesting repertory company of the twenties. He used the Dullin stage to test his own ideas. Once, out of enthusiasm for Oriental theatre, he insisted on playing a part in a Pirandello play wearing make-up that made his face look like a Chinese mask. In another role, as the bearded emperor Charlemagne, Artaud made his entrance on all fours, like a dog. "Couldn't you try to find an entrance that is a bit less stylized?" Dullin gently asked. "Ah, well, then," huffed Artaud, "if all you are interested in is realism!"

Artaud was also gaining a reputation as a film actor, although he was usually typecast as a fanatic, like Savonarola in Abel Gance's *Lucrezia Borgia* or Marat in Gance's *Napoleon* or the shell-shocked World War I soldier in the film *The Wooden Crosses*. His most important part was in Carl Dreyer's *La Passion de Jeanne d'Arc* (1928), where he played the monk who hears Joan's confession before she is burned at the stake. Artaud's grave, sensitive face is the last human face Joan sees before her death. Dreyer shot the scene entirely in close-ups and was able to restrain Artaud from his customary grimacing.

In 1924 Artaud joined the surrealists, drawn to a movement that fled the rational, sought to free the unconscious, and claimed to want to explore the secret areas of the soul. Surrealism disposed of the barrier between the real and the unreal, it repudiated traditional Western art, and it admired works as different as "Kubla Khan" and Walt Disney's *Silly Symphonies*. André Breton, the leader and "pope" of the movement, recognized in Artaud a kindred spirit and made him editor of the second and third surrealist manifestoes. Artaud was responsible for articles attacking motherhood and suggesting that all the country's prisons and barracks be emptied.

But while surrealism was revolutionary in its views, it was dictatorial in its organization, and members were constantly being read out of the movement for minor doctrinal infractions. Artaud could not survive long under such regimentation. The radical difference between Artaud and the rest of the surrealists was that they had postulated a flight from reason, while Artaud was already at the heart of unreason. He was, in a sense, the only genuine surrealist. He spent nine years in insane asylums because he was an authentic visionary, at a time when Breton was selling off his African art collection so that he could continue to live in bourgeois comfort.

Artaud's surrealist friends were dismayed by his unpredictable behavior. He once burst into the studio of the painter André Masson at dawn to demand: "Am I a better actor or poet?" Masson threw him out, but later recalled: "Artaud was our Hamlet, he was like a foreign body, a meteor, always alone." Artaud could be charming or petulant and suspicious; his friends never knew what to expect. Sitting in a café one day with the poet Jean Follain, Artaud caught sight of his name in Follain's address book. The capital A's were squared off at the top. Furious, Artaud said: "You are trying to diminish me with those A's, you are trying to blunt the sharpness of my point." Artaud had also become friendly with a promising young actor, Jean-Louis Barrault, who demonstrated his talents as a mimic by imitating him; Artaud, tearing at his hair, ran down the street shouting, "thief, thief, I've been robbed of my personality."

Artaud formed only one lasting attachment, with an actress called Genica Athanasiou, "she of the topaz eyes and the milk complexion." He lived with her on and off until 1927. For Artaud, however, sex represented the evil forces of the world against which he was struggling. He wrote that the refusal of sexuality was the refusal of compromise and complained that "sexuality is oblique, life is oblique, thought is oblique, everything is oblique."

If Artaud's private life remains mysterious, his public life was accompanied by scandal and fracas. On December 10, 1926, at 9 P.M. at the Prophet café, the surrealists met to decide whether to form an alliance with the Communist party. Artaud, for whom all political parties were equally irrelevant, displayed a noticeable lack of enthusiasm that prompted one of the left-leaning surrealists to ask: "Doesn't Artaud give a damn about the revolution?" "I don't give a damn about yours but I do give a damn about mine," Artaud said, and walked out, never to return to the surrealist fold.

Artaud now devoted himself to his own vision of the theatre. Very simply, he believed that the function of the theatre is revolutionary; a play should not entertain, it should help remake the world. The spectator should not leave the theatre yawning or smiling but shocked and terrified, like someone who has seen his wife undergo an open-heart operation or witnessed genocide in Biafra. You must go to the theatre as you would to a surgeon, insisted Artaud—gravely, knowing that you will not leave intact.

The new theatre was a revolt against French psychological drama and boulevard comedy, in which emotions and situations familiar to the audience provided a reassuring endorsement of their way of life. An authentic play, in Artaud's view, must not contribute to the audience's peace of mind but disrupt it. Traditional theatre was showing the audience the *déjà vu*, while Artaud wanted to show the *jamais vu*. On another level his theories were the result of his own estrangement. Through the medium of the theatre he wanted to transport the audience into an understanding of his torment. In 1925 he wrote a letter to the director of the Comédie Française, saying: "The theatre does not need you . . . the theatre is Tierra del Fuego, the lagoons of the sky, the battlefields of dreams, the theatre is solemnity. And you deposit your excrement at the foot of solemnity, like the Arab at the foot of the Pyramids."

Artaud operated as both a visionary and an organizer. He asked famous writers like Gide for support; he wrote puffs in the *Nouvelle Revue Française* for actresses who had promised him financial support; he indulged in the compromise and flattery familiar to French literary careerists. With the help of a fashionable hostess he organized a reading of *Richard II* for wealthy patrons of the arts. Checkbooks at the ready, they heard Artaud explain that he wanted a theatre with uncomfortable seats that would collapse if the spectators fell asleep. Foul smells, he promised, would waft through the aisles during the performance, and no accounting of the money spent would be made. Those present, he said, were Philistines and Boeotians whose last chance this was for rehabilitation. He was surprised at the meagerness of the donations and said grandly: "I did the impossible!"

Despite difficulties, many of them created by himself, Artaud founded his own company, the Alfred Jarry Theatre, named after the author of *Ubu Roi*. It lasted from 1927 to 1929 and staged a total of eight performances.

Notoriety came to the Alfred Jarry Theatre when the surrealists tried to break up a performance of Strindberg's *The Dream*, charging that Artaud had sold out by accepting subsidies from the Swedish ambassador. André Breton and his friends managed to obtain about thirty orchestra seats for the première, mingling with the Tout-Paris and prominent members of the Swedish colony. In an effort to placate his former friends Artaud announced before the curtain went up, "The action takes place in Sweden, that is to say, nowhere." At this a tall Swede rose from his seat and invited his compatriots to walk out—about ten of them did. The performance was so chaotic that Artaud asked for police

Above, Artaud plays that perennially favorite theatrical figure of madness, Marat, in Napoleon, *a French film made in 1926.*

protection on the following evenings.

The Alfred Jarry Theatre expired from lack of funds, but Artaud continued to evangelize for what he now called the Theatre of Cruelty. In 1933 there took place one of the most bizarre lectures ever given at the Sorbonne; it was Artaud discussing "The Theatre and the Plague." He was seated at a desk, with a blackboard framing his lean face. The corners of his mouth were stained black from laudanum, and when he spoke, his long-fingered hands flapped like a bird's wings, and hair fell over his massive brow. Like the plague, Artaud began, the theatre must contain the thrust of an epidemic. The plague creates a second state in which social order is abolished and the members of the community respond to deep unconscious urges; the miser throws gold out of windows, and the solemn bourgeois is seized by an erotic fever. The theatre, too, must be a crisis resolved by death or cure, it must push men to see themselves as they are. It must make the masks fall, uncover lies, baseness, and hypocrisy, and reveal to the community its dark powers and its hidden strengths.

As Artaud went on, he lost control of what he was saying and in front of his audience of Sorbonne students and intellectuals, became a victim of the plague. The American novelist Anaïs Nin, who had become friendly with Artaud and attended the lecture, described the scene in her diary: "He let

go of the thread we were following and began to act out dying by plague . . . his face contorted with anguish, and sweat dampening his hair, his eyes dilated, his muscles cramped, his fingers struggling to retain their flexibility, he made you feel the burning throat, the pains, the fever, the fire in the gut."

The audience laughed at the impromptu performance, and many left. Artaud told Anaïs Nin: "They want to hear an objective lecture on the Theatre and the Plague and I want to give them the experience itself, so they will be terrified, and awaken. I want to awaken them. They do not realize they are dead."

Friendship with Artaud, Anaïs Nin found, was at times unsettling. Sitting in the Coupole with her, he would insist that he was really the mad Roman emperor Heliogabalus. "Between us there could be a murder," he would say, and "what a divine joy it would be to crucify a being like you, who are so evanescent, so elusive." Or, he would discuss his illness and say: "I have known only painful emotions. I have chosen the domain of pain and shadows as others choose the radiance and weight of matter."

Despite the pain and the shadows he went on to write his manifesto for the Theatre of Cruelty, a text that later appeared with four or five other articles in a book called *The Theatre and Its Double*, and that has been called by Robert Brustein, dean of the Yale Drama School, "one of the most influential, as well as one of the most inflammatory, documents of our time." Unlike the other great theorist of the twentieth-century theatre, Bertolt Brecht, Artaud was not himself a gifted dramatist who could write vehicles for his ideas. Nor did he have a laboratory like the Berliner Ensemble. Brecht built up an *oeuvre* that perpetuated his doctrine; Artaud must be seen as a prophet announcing a new theatrical age.

By cruelty, Artaud said, he meant "not the cruelty we can exercise against one another . . . but the much more necessary and terrible cruelty that things can exercise against us. We are not free. And the sky can fall on our heads. And the theatre exists first to teach us that . . . I propose to return the theatre to this magic and elementary idea, picked up by modern psychoanalysis, which consists, to heal the sick, in making them adopt the external attitude of the state to which they should be brought."

If all this sounds a trifle murky, it is precisely because it is the poetic vision of a man who passionately believed that society could be changed through the privileged art form of the theatre, rather than through a list of stage directions. In his revolt against the kind of theatre that tells a story, with the actors on one side and the audience on the other, Artaud did away with the conventional script and the conventional stage. In the most intense situations, he said, words are inadequate and are replaced by screams or gestures. Thus, language is unimportant. Words should be used more for their vibratory quality than for what they represent. Instead of a stage Artaud wanted to use a hangar or a loft, the way churches were used for Passion plays. The spectator would sit in the middle, enveloped by the play and the actors; scenes would start like fires at different points of the hall and would also spread like fires. There should be no written plays; they were to be replaced by mythical themes, like the story of Bluebeard or the Capture of Jerusalem, situations full of violence and movement that would contain the necessary dose of cruelty. As for the actor, his main requirement should be proper breathing; he must be what Artaud called "an athlete of the senses." The essential dramatic problem, however, should always be how to take a spatial unit and make it eloquent, "like mines in a rock cliff that bring forth geysers."

Artaud's Theatre of Cruelty is an ideal theatre that was never meant to be staged, just as Plato's writings on democracy could never serve as the platform for any administration, Republican or Democrat. Artaud never bothered to explain how to obtain the eloquence of language without language or how to maintain dramatic coherence without the focus of a stage. Following his instructions to the letter would lead to a kind of solemn pandemonium, like *Hellzapoppin* without the jokes.

But precisely because it is an ideal theatre, it has, like a religion, given birth to several diverse sects. The Living Theatre is the most obviously Artaud-inspired troupe. Its co-director Judith Malina calls Artaud "my madman muse." Living Theatre actors leave the stage, wander among the audience, and writhe in the aisles in Artaud-like torment. They separate language from its meaning and give it an incantatory value, as in the barked Marine commands of *The Brig*. They, too, believe that the theatre can transform society. Less directly derived from Artaud but sharing common attitudes are Jean Genet's plays, with their insistence on the ceremonial and the blasphemous, their need to shock the audience, and their revolt against bourgeois values. Jerzy Grotowski's bizarre Polish Laboratory Theatre, in which spectators are likely to watch ritual slaughters in a theatre designed to resemble a miniature coliseum, is another Artaud-inspired troupe. Finally, the English director Peter Brook has acknowledged his debt to Artaud. His staging of *Marat/Sade* is an aggression on the spectator, and here again there is a confusion between actors and audience, with the inference that madness is contagious. Outside the theatre, Artaud could probably claim some responsibility for today's permanent spirit of youthful revolt and for the refuge youth movements have taken in drugs and magic and gospels, like the *I Ching* and *The Tibetan Book of the Dead*.

The closest Artaud came to staging the Theatre of Cruelty was his 1935 production of *The Cenci*, a melodrama of murder and incest in an Italian Renaissance family that was derived from Shelley's tragedy and from the *Italian Chronicles* of Stendhal. Artaud himself said that there was as much difference between *The Cenci* and the Theatre of Cruelty as there was between a water fountain and a thunderstorm. With Artaud playing the incestuous father, *The Cenci* ran for seventeen performances in a run-down theatre called the Folies-Wagram at the end of a dead-end street. Artaud practiced his theories concerning screams, gestures, and the use of lighting as a language, but the critics were not impressed. They repeated what had already been said of Alfred Jarry: "He may have genius, too bad he has no talent." The Tout-Paris laughed at the man who had bought a ticket to *The Cenci* thinking it was a team of Italian acrobats.

Despondent over the reception of *The Cenci*, Artaud left for Mexico in January, 1936, to look for a tribe of Indians called the Tarahumaras, which he had heard still practiced Aztec sun rites and used the hallucinatory drug peyote. Armed with a *laissez-passer* from the Mexican minister of education and accompanied by a half-breed interpreter-guide, Artaud made his way into the Mexican sierra and found the Tarahumaras, who were living, he said, "in a prediluvian state . . . they believed they have been dropped from the sky onto the sierra . . . they sometimes visit the cities in order to see those who went wrong!" Artaud unfortunately arrived during a government crackdown on the peyote-eaters and had to wait some time before he could attend the rites, but when he did, he said: "I felt I had reached a capital point of my existence." As he watched the Indians perform a dance called the Ciguri, Artaud was given some peyote by a priest. It was, he said, "enough peyote to see God two or three times." He felt his mind leaving his body through his various organs, and when he was himself again, the Indians told him that his "skeleton had returned from the dark rite, like the night marching on the night." Describing the difference between opium and peyote, Artaud wrote: "the first virtue of opium is to allow us to grasp reality, without delirium or hallucination, but with balance and thoughtfulness, while peyote makes intelligence futile and returns us to life purged after a phase of trances."

Returning to France early in 1937, Artaud relied so heavily on drugs that he twice had to take the cure, with his friend Jean Paulhan from the *Nouvelle Revue Française* footing some of the bills. He also managed to get engaged to a Belgian girl named Cécile Schramme, whose father operated the Brussels streetcar line. But the engagement was broken off after Artaud had a violent quarrel with his fiancée's family during a visit to Brussels.

After his Mexican adventure Artaud longed to visit other cultures that still believed in magic. A Dutch surrealist had given him an ancient cane with thirteen knots, and he convinced himself it was the magic cane that had belonged to Saint Patrick. He decided to go to Ireland to return the cane and look for traces of druidic rites in the Aran Islands. Arriving in Dublin in the summer of 1937, he wrote a postcard to a friend that said: "My life is the realization of a prophecy." Thereafter his letters grew increasingly oracular. In September he wrote André Breton that a horrible uprising was being fomented against him by the forces of high capitalism, but that the woman who had organized it would be publicly massacred. The letter was decorated with cabalistic signs, rows of numbers, and strange drawings. Out of funds, Artaud sought asylum in a Dublin monastery, but the monks were in retreat, and alarmed by this wild-eyed fellow with long stringy hair like a nineteenth-century violinist, they called the police when he made a scene. He

was arrested and deported to France on a ship called the *Washington*. Jean Paulhan, not having heard from him in some time, wrote the French legation in Dublin and received the following reply: "Monsieur Artaud's presence in Dublin was mentioned to the legation by the Irish police, who expressed the desire to send our compatriot back to France because he had no funds and demonstrated a great exaltation."

What happened aboard the *Washington* remains unclear. Artaud later said he was in his cabin peacefully looking out the porthole at the sea when a steward and the chief mechanic, who was carrying a monkey wrench, burst in and attacked him. Considering the tone of his letters from Ireland and his arrest by the Irish police, it seems possible that he suffered some sort of seizure aboard ship. In any case, alone and cut off from the friends who were usually around to help him, he was tied up and committed to an insane asylum when the ship landed at Le Havre. His head was shaved, and he was forced to wear the gray uniform of state asylums. His personal belongings, manuscripts, and notes were taken away from him and later mysteriously disappeared.

Artaud remained convinced that his return to Le Havre had prompted an uprising to prevent him from making important declarations and that the surrealist leader André Breton had been killed coming to his rescue. "I never contradicted him," recalled Breton. "I changed the subject—finally one day at the Deux Magots he asked me to confirm what he was saying [that Breton was dead and resurrected] and I had to admit that on that point my recollections were different from his own. He looked at me in despair and tears clouded his eyes. But soon he was smiling again—he realized that occult powers had managed to befuddle me."

Artaud was moved from asylum to asylum. He was all but forgotten by his friends, who had more urgent concerns in those troubled prewar years, and his

family did nothing to obtain his release. His first letters were sent after a year and a half of internment. "I am not a madman," he wrote, "I am a fanatic—I deliberately had myself locked up so I could carry out the prophecies of Saint Patrick."

In 1943, thanks to the efforts of the poet Robert Desnos, Artaud was transferred to a private psychiatric hospital in the peaceful south-central French town of Rodez. He could come and go in the town as he liked, and he spent many hours praying in the cathedral. But his psychiatrist, Doctor Ferdière, while lenient, believed that Artaud's delirium made him violent, antisocial, and dangerous to public order. Ferdière treated him with electroshocks that took on, for Artaud, the aspect of a torture to make him give up his visions and accept the rational world of other men. Artaud recounted that when he told Ferdière he was controlled by demons, Ferdière said:

"Now Monsieur Artaud, I'm afraid you are getting delirious again."

"What do you mean delirious, I am quoting you fact and I can show you proof."

"You are obstinate in your delirium, we will have to start a new series of shock treatments and I will write your friend Jean Paulhan that I have had to resort to them again."

"But I'm not the only writer who has mentioned sorcery. Read Huysmans in *Là Bas* . . ."

"Huysmans was as crazy as you are, and all those who believed in the beyond were mad, like Nietzsche and Gérard de Nerval. There has never been scientific proof of scorcery, and if you remain so stubborn you will have to stay in this asylum for the rest of your life."

If Artaud is to be believed, the good doctor's therapy consisted of using electroshock as a form of punishment and reminding Artaud each day that he was hopelessly insane. Artaud felt that the doctor was an implacable enemy and that it was essential for him to prove the validity of his therapeutic system by making Artaud admit that he did not really have visions. Each electroshock treatment plunged Artaud into terror, and the thought of those to come plunged him into despair. In a self-portrait of that period he sketched himself with a nose devoured by vermin, with the right eye an empty socket and the left eye asymmetrical, and without a mouth. "If I have no mouth," he explained, "then I have no teeth, no larynx, no esophagus, no stomach, and no anus."

With the war over, friends could visit him again and take steps to obtain his release. In 1946 Doctor Ferdière agreed to release him in their custody if they would guarantee his livelihood. A benefit auction was held at the Sarah Bernhardt theatre, and the paintings and manuscripts sold netted Artaud one million francs. He moved to a rest home in the Paris suburb of Ivry, where he was a guest, not an inmate. He still believed he had magic powers. Once when the concierge in a friend's building in Paris took exception to his shouting the verses of Gérard de Nerval out an open window, Artaud told her: "Be quiet—if you persist in preventing me from reading poetry I am going to turn you into a flat-headed serpent."

Artaud showed that as a free man he was able to function and work. He had done no writing during his nine years in asylums, but now in a few days of inspired activity he wrote a short book about Van Gogh, the work of one illuminé about another. Like himself, Van Gogh had been committed. The Dutch painter, Artaud wrote, had been driven both to mutilation and to suicide by a society that was sick: "A doomed society invented psychiatry as a smoke screen . . . what is an authentic lunatic? A man who preferred to go mad, in the social sense of the word, rather than forfeit a certain superior idea of human honor . . . and a man whom society wants to prevent from telling unbearable truths."

The Van Gogh book won the Sainte-Beuve prize for the best critical work

of 1947, but Artaud's next effort was less successful. He was invited to record a radio broadcast, but the director of the French radio network banned it. The program, called "To end god's judgment," began with this alarming bit of information: "I learned yesterday of/one of the most sensational official practices in/American state schools which no doubt makes that country/think itself in the forefront of progress./Apparently among the examinations and tests which a child/is made to undergo when it first enters a state school,/is the so-called test of the seminal liquid or sperm/which consists of asking this newly enrolled child for a/little of its sperm in order to put in a flask,/and to keep it ready in this way for all attempts at/artificial insemination which might take place . . ." The Americans, he noted, are using every expedient to manufacture soldiers for eventual interplanetary war.

He concluded by suggesting, "Now it is man we must decide to emasculate/at this time. . . ./By putting him once more, but the last time,/on the autopsy table so as to reconstitute his anatomy. . . ./Man is sick because he is badly made./We must decide to lay him bare so we can/scratch this insect for him, which itches him to death . . ."

For Artaud, however, it was too late for corporal change or for the operating table. He looked so ravaged that a friend took him to the Salpetrière hospital, where specialists diagnosed cancer of the rectum, but did not tell him. A year before his death he gave his last major performance. On January 13, 1947, seven hundred persons crowded into the tiny Théâtre du Vieux Colombier to hear Artaud lecture. The two Andrés were there, Breton and Gide, as well as Albert Camus and a score of other writers whose presence showed that Artaud's books, although published in small numbers, were steadily making their way. But much of the audience had probably been drawn by the promise of seeing a freak, like the man with

the crocodile skin or the tattooed lady in the circus.

Artaud did indeed look like a fugitive from a side show, a grimacing phantom of a man—toothless, emaciated, ragged, his disorderly hair tumbling about his shoulders, his eyes filled with the same panic that he had simulated years before in the part of the shell-shocked soldier. But once he began to speak, those present realized that they were not going to be entertained, but that Artaud had placed them in the uncomfortable position of watching a man live out his torment. This was the Theatre of Cruelty: to see Artaud stutter, sob, and shout as he told about his treatment in asylums and made them reflect on a society that could produce an individual at once so lucid and so demented. Suddenly he stopped, the fire subsided, and he said very calmly: "I put myself in your place and I see that what I am saying is devoid of interest—how can I be really sincere?"

To deaden his pain, Artaud took heavy doses of laudanum and chloral, and he spent much of the last year of his life nodding out. The body he had loathed was taking its vengeance. In February, 1948, he wrote his friend Paule Thévenin: "There are those who eat too much, and those like myself who can no longer eat without vomiting." A week later, on the morning of March 4, the gardener of the Ivry rest home brought Artaud his breakfast as usual and found him dead at the foot of the bed, clutching a shoe.

With his death, his legend grew. More than twenty years later Artaud endures as a cult figure. His complete works are being published by Gallimard, the Theatre of Cruelty continues to inspire a certain kind of modern drama, and madness itself is understood in some circles today as a form of artistic sensibility.

Sanche de Gramont is the author of The French, *a Book-of-the-Month-Club selection last year. He is now living in Tangier, where he is at work on a novel.*

Daedalus and I

A noted sculptor tells how he re-created
an ancient labyrinth—and got caught in it. Is he,
in fact, the father of Icarus reincarnate?

I have been a traveler across time, first by chance and then by choice, and for some time with no choice. Once you are in, you are in: if you make a myth your matrix and if that myth is centered upon as ancient and potent a concept as the Labyrinth, you build it around yourself without becoming aware that you are lost in the thing. Finding your way out only takes you deeper in, and only the way in is the way out.

Since May 11, 1956, when I stood on the point at Procida, west of Naples, and looked down the long isthmus toward the great rock of Cumae, which towers over the sea and the Pallid Lake, I have lived among the "wandering ways," as Virgil called them, deep in the second millennium B.C. and no less deep in the twentieth century A.D., because, in a maze, time crosses and recrosses and one time lives in another. If I can escape I shall, but whenever in fourteen years I have felt that I have said what I had to say about Daedalus, the Athenian who built the Cretan Labyrinth, and Icarus, his son, who flew with him and fell from flight, something has occurred that has given me more to know and more to do in sculpture and painting and more to say in

In his studio in Essex, Michael Ayrton adjusts a bronze sketch for his Daedalus-Icarus Matrix. *The final version of the work (pages 62–63) was later installed in a mirrored chamber of the huge maze built to Ayrton's design on a New York estate.*

words. Myth lengthens and thickens, coiling like a labyrinth around itself.

I began my wandering in the myth of Daedalus by making a wash drawing of the acropolis of Cumae, a sacred place colonized by the Greeks from Euboea about 800 B.C., and before that a trading post that was known to the Mycenaeans, and before that the place where Daedalus landed at the end of his long flight. None of this I knew when I made the drawing. I walked along the isthmus in the heat of the day and went into the labyrinth of passages that honeycomb the great rock. From the center of this place the Cumaean Sibyl spoke her oracles. The voice of Apollo spoke through her, and what she said came to be set down in books that the Romans kept to consult in times of crisis, in the Temple of Capitoline Jove. Aeneas spoke to her, pausing on his voyage from burned and vanquished Troy, and went down through her maze of caves to Lake Avernus and into the underworld to seek advice from his father. Her voice was heard across the sea and across the landscape in "a hundred rushing streams of sound" through "a hundred mouth openings" in the rock.

Hearing them in the silence of my mind and commanded by the long-inhabited and numinous place, I obeyed. For fourteen years it has been the center of my focus, and what began as one wash drawing grew this year into a maze of brick and stone with 1,680 feet of wandering pathways and

walls six and eight feet high. This year, too, it shrank to a honeycomb in gold, four inches across, inhabited by seven golden bees.

Virgil recounts the outline of the myth of Daedalus in Book VI of the *Aeneid,* describing the reliefs that Daedalus cast for the great temple to Apollo that he founded on the summit of the Cumaean rock.

Daedalus when he was in flight from the tyranny of Minos adventured his life in the sky on swooping wings and glided toward the chill north by tracks unknown. At last he hovered lightly above the Euboean stronghold. In these lands he first found refuge and straightway consecrated the oarage of his wings to Phoebus Apollo for whom he founded a gigantic temple. "On the temple gate he pictured . . . the island on which Knossos stands, rising high above the sea . . . the Bull's brutal passion, and Pasiphaë's secret union with him and the record of wicked love, hybrid procreation, two shapes in one, the Minotaur in the midst of the winding ways of the house that was there, which might not be unraveled except that the Builder himself pitied the queen . . . and guiding sightless footsteps with his thread unlocked the coils. And Icarus, he too would have found prominence on this great sculpture but for the power of grief: for Daedalus twice seeking to mold his fall in gold had twice failed."

To Virgil's audience further parts of the legend would have been familiar.

By MICHAEL AYRTON

In 1956 Ayrton sketched the ruined city of Cumae (center background), the first Greek colony in Italy and home of the Cumaean Sibyl. According to Virgil, Daedalus landed here after his flight.

They would have known how Daedalus left the little kingdom of Athens and took service with Minos, who ruled Crete from the city of Knossos, the center of the first great European civilization. They would have known how he built for Minos and what marvels he made with the tools that he invented, among them the saw, the auger, the plumb line, tongs, and the ball-and-socket joint, for Daedalus was the archetype of architects, inventors, and technicians. They would have known how the craftsman Daedalus contrived the lifelike simulacrum of a cow in which Pasiphaë crouched to receive the white bull who mated with her, and how Minos blamed the craftsman for this contrivance and locked him with Icarus in the Labyrinth Daedalus himself had made to imprison the bull-headed man, the Minotaur, and hide the hybrid evidence of the queen's lust. It was there, in the Labyrinth, that Daedalus made wings for himself and for Icarus, upon which they were the first men to fly, and on that flight Icarus flew too near the sun so that his wings melted and he fell to his death in the sea. They would have known, too, how Daedalus landed at Cumae and built the temple to Apollo, who had killed his son, and how he thereafter journeyed to Sicily, where Minos pursued him, and how he killed Minos and went from Sicily to Sardinia, taking his genius as a metalworker to that island where perhaps he died. They would have known the myth as an amalgam of many variations on a theme, some in harmony, some in conflict, for that is what myth is. It is not simple, it grows and reshapes itself continually.

Virgil wrote of this legend, as did Ovid, Plutarch, and Diodorus Siculus and before them the Greek poets Epimenides, Bacchylides, Cleidemus, and Philochorus, in relation to the parallel myth of Theseus, which joins and crosses the myth of Daedalus, who was Theseus's kinsman. Fourteen hundred years after Virgil and before Bruegel painted his *Fall of Icarus*, Chaucer wrote briefly of Daedalus and his son;

Shakespeare speaks of them in *Henry VI*, as does Goethe in *Faust*. In modern times James Joyce's hero is Stephen Dedalus; Picasso and Matisse have painted Icarus; and Gide's *Theseus*, his last major work, is centered on the Cretan Labyrinth. Daedalus is alive, as he was alive before Homer wrote of him in the *Iliad*. I know. I have lived with him, and like those who have told and retold the narrative and portrayed the events, I have added what was given me to add and reshaped the legend where I had need to do so.

What began for me with the landscape of Cumae continued in the landscape of Greece and the islands. It was on Crete in 1958 that Daedalus became specific to me, a man in whose life I was inextricably involved. I began to know him and sense his uneasy relationship with his son. I made bronzes of them. Daedalus in turn, seemingly, was engaged upon making the wings somewhere in the Maze at Knossos. In 1959 I began to concentrate on the flight itself and the sea over which they flew, and these things emerged in paint and collage, in drawings and sculpture.

In 1960 I wrote a short narrative called *The Testament of Daedalus*, which told of the flight. On the day I corrected the proofs, a man won a prize for making the first man-powered flight since Daedalus and Icarus. It seemed odd, but then, for about twenty-five centuries after the origins of the legend flight itself had been treated as a fantasy or a folly. It is not now, nor has it been since 1905; and it is a measure of the god's irony that the first air-borne invasion ever to take place should have led to the capture of Crete in 1941. As the stress of that first flight became clearer to me, so the parallel between the myth and the facts of our own time became more explicit. The head and then the whole figure of Icarus reshaped itself, and he evolved into something as remote as an astronaut and yet was piercingly immediate in his relevance to me as a human being under stress.

At this point the other dramatis personae of the myth began to pull at me down the passages of the Maze: Minos the king and his queen Pasiphaë; Tauros, their military commander; Talos, the bronze man, a technician turned into a metallic warrior to become guardian of Crete. I made images of him before I knew he had been Daedalus's nephew, but that can happen if you visit with so remote a family. The Minotaur came sharply into my foreground in 1962 and began the agonized evolution toward the human condition that to me is his nature and his ambition. Him I drew and cast in bronze, but I never painted him. I do not know why. It has been said that Theseus slew the Minotaur, but Theseus was a braggart, and the Minotaur is killed every Sunday in Spain or Mexico, and as Picasso knows, he does not die. Icarus does nothing else.

I went back to Cumae, having been to Delphi, and the Sibyl demanded to be made in bronze in fifteen different forms. She too was a relative both of her Delphic counterpart, the Pythian oracle, and of Queen Pasiphaë: the female factor in myth is no less powerful than it is in life. But finally Daedalus himself came to dominate the Maze, and by then I had identified myself with him so compulsively that the myth began to reshape itself, expanding in my mind, and without any warning I found myself writing a further narrative, a transposed autobiography.

I did this to complete a jigsaw, or rather, to find a way out of the myth itself. I believed that if I could add to the sum of all the images I had made a narrative that would place them, would assemble the mass of fragments that all my work in painting and sculpture seemed to be, I might see the Labyrinth of Daedalus clearly and escape from it. I took two years to write *The Maze Maker,** and the publishers called it a novel. During all that time I made drawings, paintings, and sculptures on the theme of the Maze Maker. It was no use: I was not out, I was deeper in. I had written the whole "autobiography" of Daedalus to rid myself of him, and I had produced in fact the exact reverse of an illustrated book, for all the images preceded it or continued to emerge while I was writing, and the text did no more for me than explain what I was doing in there. Furthermore, I became entangled in the long, complicated, and curious history, prehistory, and meaning of mazes, which begins at least five thousand years ago.

In the ancient world great labyrinths were built of stone. Herodotus described the labyrinth of Egypt built by the pharaoh Amenenhat III as consisting of three thousand intercommuni-

*Holt, Rinehart & Winston, 1967; paperback edition, Bantam Books.

cating rooms on two levels, while Pliny wrote of a maze on the island of Lemnos built on the Egyptian pattern and renowned for the beauty of its one hundred and fifty columns. There was another maze on Samos, said to have been built by Theodorus, and one at Chiusi, of which Marcus Terentius Varro gives a detailed if improbable account. This Etruscan maze lay underground, below the tomb of Lars Porsena of Clusium, and it was inextricable "to anyone who entered it without a clue of thread." That clue of thread derives from the red one Ariadne gave to Theseus so that he might find his way in the Cretan Labyrinth built by Daedalus.

None of these vast buildings has survived. What we have are heraldic versions of the Cretan Maze on coins of Knossos from the fifth to the first century B.C.; ideograms of even earlier date, going back to Minoan times, which derived from the maze and were painted on the walls of houses, found their way into textiles and were incised upon funerary urns. Their purpose was to protect, and the "meander," or "key," pattern is one of them.

In Roman times mazes took the form of mosaic floor motifs and even passed into children's games, where they have remained to this day. Pliny referred to them as *"in pavimentis puerorumve ludicris campestribus."* They have come down to us modified into hopscotch, which calls to mind the floor maze mentioned in Book XVIII of Homer's *Iliad.* Upon the shield made by the bronzesmith god Hephaestus for the warrior Achilles, there was depicted, among other things, "a dancing floor like the one Daedalus designed in the spacious town of Knossos for Ariadne of the lovely locks." Homer does not specifically refer to a maze, but there is other evidence that the pattern laid out for Ariadne was a plan of the intricate maneuvers required of the dancers imitating the mating ceremony of the crane or the partridge. In this dance, called the *geranos,* the complicated circling, advance, and withdrawal from the female

at the center practiced by the male may originally have been totemic or possibly mimetic, to insure success in the hunt. It is Ariadne's dance that Theseus is said to have learned from Daedalus and danced at the entrance to the Labyrinth, and in the twelfth century A.D. the learned monk Eustathius of Thessalonica related this part of the legend, recalling an old man on Delos who remembered the steps.

In the ancient world everything meant both itself and something else. A ritual devised for one purpose could come to represent another, and the *geranos* relates to the maze, since the maze itself is concerned with a complicated circling passage to the center. It is a coil. In ritual the *geranos* threaded its way through that coil to act out the climax of the dance.

The function of the maze is twofold: to arrest the intruder by confusing him, and to protect the center from intrusion. As a fortification it embodied the principle of the enfilade, without which the trench warfare of World War I could not have been conducted with guns nor the Iron Age Maiden Castle have been defended with spears and arrows. Those who sought to enter sought to kill.

The Maze at Knossos, as Virgil describes it, is wholly different from Homer's dancing floor. Virgil's labyrinth was a palace with high walls and "wandering ways" through which Theseus was guided by Ariadne's thread. The Maze at Knossos had been built by Daedalus to imprison the Minotaur, and from it he and his son had escaped (like cranes or partridges) by flying out. It is in fact in Virgil's *Aeneid* that the version of the myth still familiar to us is to be found. However, Virgil also describes a dance or game—*Ludus Trojae*—that was performed by young Trojans at the funeral games for Anchises and at the foundation of Alba Longa. The exact origins of this tradition are lost, but an Etruscan wine-jug of the seventh century B.C. carries a graffito that shows a maze from which

Daedalus Head *(1959–60, 12½" high) is one of "perhaps three hundred drawings, fifteen bronzes, a group of reliefs in various media, and a dozen or so paintings" that the author produced between 1958 and 1962, "all centered on that epic flight" of Daedalus and his ill-fated son, Icarus. Several examples of Ayrton's work appear here.*

emerges a line of warriors both mounted and on foot, and the maze is clearly labeled *truia*. This is one among many indications that a myth or rite that associated Troy with a maze and with a dance existed at least eight hundred years before Virgil wrote. There is other early evidence to suggest that the defense of walled cities involved maze rituals. Joshua's circling of the walls of Jericho, which caused them to fall, coincides with the ancient convention that a maze has seven turns or seven "decision points" at which the intruder must decide between alternative routes. If Joshua marched his army seven times around Jericho counter to the original foundation ritual of that city, the maze defenses would be unwound, and the city could fall, as it is described as doing, to the conqueror.

There is a further symbolism of great importance and of even greater antiquity than the Homeric or Virgilian legends. This is to be found in the Sumerian epic of Gilgamesh, which exists in various Mesopotamian tongues and is at least a thousand years older than the occurrences on Crete relayed to us by Homer and Virgil. In the Gilgamesh Epic the Sumerian hero seeks to find his way through a cedar forest (a place of terror to the inhabitant of an alluvial plain devoid of trees of any sort). This labyrinth-like forest is ruled by the entrail demon Humbaba, and Gilgamesh succeeds in find-

ing his way through the forest and killing the demon. Thereafter Gilgamesh rejects the goddess Ishtar, much as Theseus rejected and abandoned Ariadne on Naxos. Rahab the harlot, on the other hand, was not rejected after she had betrayed Jericho to the Jews and assisted their entry with a red cord. The red cord hung from the window was the sign that she should be spared. In the epic of Gilgamesh, the entrail demon of the forest maze, whose image survives in a Babylonian terra cotta of the seventh century B.C., is represented as himself a maze: his head is a complex pattern of intertwined entrails. Now the Akkadian word *ekkalu* means either "palace" or "temple" (as does the Hebrew word *heichal*), and Akkadian is among the earliest decipherable Mesopotamian languages. The word was used in the practice of augury, or divination from the entrails of sacrificial animals, to mean "the palace of the intestines" and seems also to have been synonymous with the Mesopotamian word for the underworld. What is more, other Akkadian divinatory terms seem to have been elaborate metaphors in which parts of the entrails were represented as "mountains," "rivers," "passages," etc., or, in effect, a description of landscape. The liver, by which the form of divination called haruspicy was practiced, seems, together with the entrails, to have symbolized the Mesopotamian universe. Augury and haruspicy both continued into Roman times. Thus, by implication, man contained the image of the universe within himself from the third millennium B.C. until the practice of animal sacrifice ceased in the Christian world and the metaphor lost some of its physical significance.

It did not, however, die out. It was modified to mean the symbolic passage through life and death into redemption. As such it is believed to have been embroidered on the robes of Byzantine emperors, and by the twelfth century A.D. it had become a

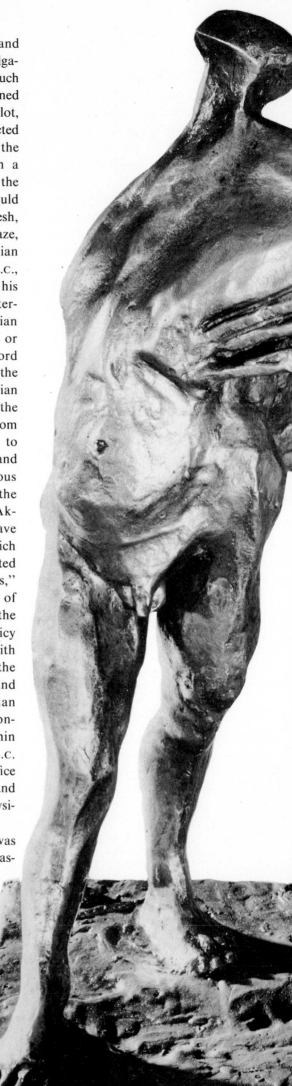

Daedalus I, *1959–60, 16" high*

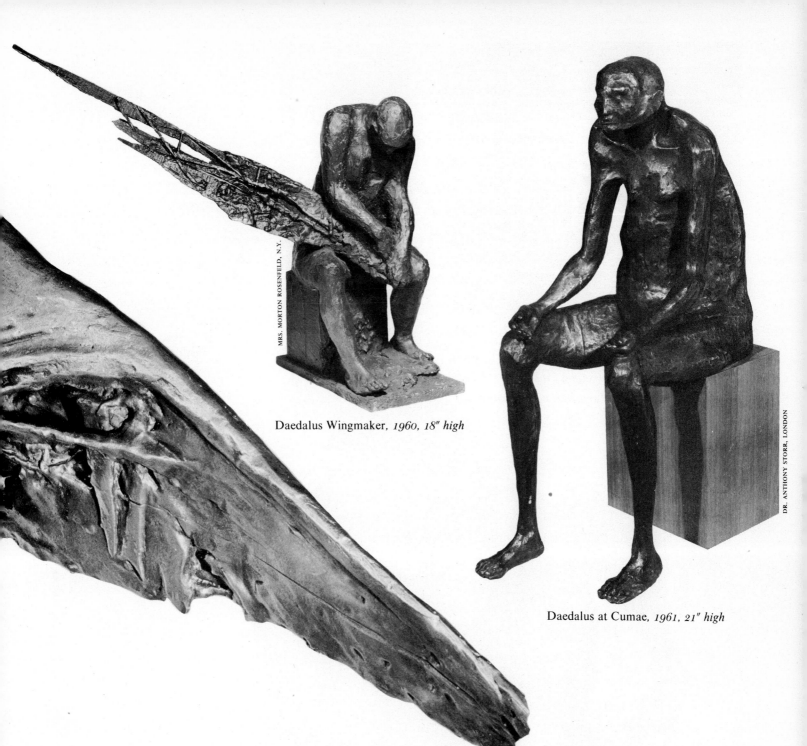

Daedalus Wingmaker, *1960, 18" high*

Daedalus at Cumae, *1961, 21" high*

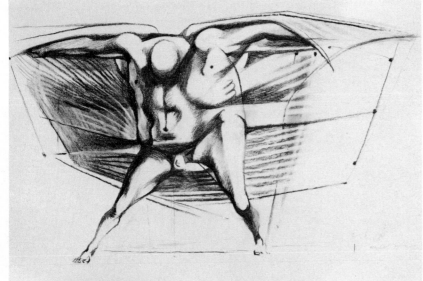

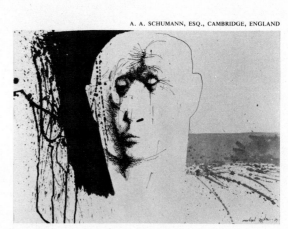

Daedalus Head I, *1959, pen and wash*

Daedalus Winged, *1961, charcoal*

PHOTOGRAPH BURTON BERINSKY; BELOW: GRAHAM FINLAYSON

After writing The Maze Maker, *Ayrton became one himself when a Wall Street financier, Armand G. Erpf, asked him to design this labyrinth for his estate in the Catskills. Its 1,680 feet of brick-walled passageways lead to two inner chambers containing the figures shown below and at right. It is probably the biggest and certainly the most expensive labyrinth since that of King Minos.*

Minotaur, *6' 6" high*

Daedalus-Icarus Matrix, *8' high*

floor pattern once more, a dancing floor of pain where those who had failed in their vows to go on pilgrimage traversed it on their knees in penitence. Such a maze, forty feet in diameter, survives in the nave of the Chartres cathedral, but unlike the maze of Daedalus, the Jerusalem, or medieval, maze contains no traps or false leads. Those who patiently traverse every coil will reach the center, and that center was called *Le Ciel*. On the other hand, at Amiens there was a floor maze that contained the names of all the master builders of the cathedral, woven into the coil. Thus was Daedalus remembered as the archetypal architect, and thus his name appears in an inscription beside the twelfth-century maze in the wall of the cathedral at Lucca.

From the church the maze moved out into the garden, and topiary mazes, of which the most famous is the one planted at Hampton Court Palace in 1690, became a common feature in formal gardens. In my local town of Saffron Walden there were three mazes: one in the church, a medieval "turf maze" cut in a field, and a topiary maze in a garden, but I knew nothing to speak of about any kind of maze until I went into the rock at Cumae. I knew none of their history until I began, in 1964, to write *The Maze Maker;* but perhaps because, like every human being, I contained a maze, I found that I wrote of the labyrinth below the rock of Cumae as the entrails of the Earth and believed, as Daedalus would have done, that the Earth was female. Her name in Greek is Gaia. The whole of the central part of the book takes place below the rock of Cumae, and in writing it, the idea came to me that the maze, which is a natural place of terror, a convolution of dark caves and buried passages, must have originated inside the belly of man and his animal prey. As a symbol, in its most profound and ancient form, the inexplicable yards of intertwining intestine that man first

revealed when he inserted his flint knife into his victim were the source of his awe and the potency of the image. The complex of guts would have been inexplicable, and that his children were formed somewhere in the passages and chambers within the female body would have been part of the mystery. When a child was born from his woman, it was joined to her by a red thread, by Ariadne's thread. This I divined; the evidence of Sumerian divination and other recondite matters, I learned later.

When Daedalus went into the earth at Cumae under oath to build a temple to Apollo, he was faced with technical problems, and since it was he who wrote *The Maze Maker,* he had need to explain them, for where most myths are the work of poets who deal in the miraculous, Daedalus is a technician who deals with the practical. Thus he reports that under the rock at Cumae lived a race of metalworkers, craftsmen who, like the Cretan Dactyli whose name means "finger men," lived secretly and apart. Such peoples in the ancient world were either dwarfs, like the Cabeiri, or giants, like the Cyclopes who toiled under Mount Etna. Those under Cumae were small men who never revealed their names, and only one could speak Greek. To enlist the aid of this man (whom he calls "the Greek Speaker") and his fellow craftsmen, Daedalus had to convince them of his mastery. He chose to make a perfect honeycomb in gold as an offering to the Earth Mother, and this he did, according to Diodorus Siculus, although Diodorus places the event at Eryx in Sicily. As an achievement this honeycomb remained a mystery and a marvel for two thousand years, since Diodorus, writing in the first century B.C., did not suggest how it was done, and what is more impossibly fragile to make in metal than a honeycomb?

Since Daedalus dictated *The Maze Maker,* he could hardly leave matters so vague, and since metalwork is part of my trade, too, he revealed the secret to me when I came to write down his words. I quote him:

"To cast a honeycomb in gold is not easy, but it is less difficult than it might appear. I shall explain why and reveal a small mystery, one of those upon which my fame rests, for it was this task successfully accomplished which bound the small people to me and made the construction of Apollo's temple possible.

"I asked for a perfect piece of comb from a well-kept hive and after much delay, it was brought to me. I asked for privacy, saying that I must invoke the gods' aid with secret charms, and my demand was treated respectfully, for all metalworkers hedge their craft about with mystification. I was taken to a small but adequate cave and there supplied with wax, fire, tools, a bench, a kiln, bellows, and all the necessary impedimenta of the goldsmith.

"Fist to forehead, I invoked the Mother and the small men reverently withdrew. It was important that they should, for I gambled on their failure to make a simple connection between the craft of lost-wax casting and the nature of the honeycomb itself. Honey is sacred to the earth goddess and wax comes from the honeycomb. With wax men make the models cast in bronze, as I have described. The small people had given me a honeycomb but they had also given me wax to make my model. Thus I knew that they had not made the connection. They had not realized that the honeycomb itself, being of wax, is the only creation in nature which is itself a wax model and one more delicately constructed than any a man could achieve.

"I ignored the wax I had been given and took the comb. It was necessary to uncap the individual cells and to do this I cut laterally through the comb and drained out the honey. Each cell of comb I now filled with fine ground clay and rock dust in a paste as thin as cream new risen on a pan of milk, so that each cell was filled with core. To the side of the whole piece of comb I attached a tiny pouring cup and thin 'runners' of wax. It was solely for the pouring cup and vents that I used the separate wax I had been given. Then, I mantled the whole and when all was hardened in the kiln, I burnt out the waxen comb.

"Gold pours thin and quickly. I poured each section while the core was still hot and the gold could run smoothly, and so the honeycomb was cast. Breaking the crust and tapping out the core was long and delicate labor, but in time I had the golden comb clean and had covered all its faults with gold granulations to resemble drops of honey. Finally, I capped some of the cells to emphasize the structure. . . .

"I covered my work and called the Greek Speaker. 'Send for seven bees,' I said with heavy solemnity, 'for without them the golden comb will never fill with honey.'

"He went away and by whatever means, at that time not known to me, he made communication with the world outside and in due time brought me seven bees, workers from the same hive as the comb I had been given as a model. Of this he solemnly assured me. Left alone, I made sacrifice to Artemis of these seven bees.

"There is another trick of casting which I was certain would not be known to the small people and it is this. Anything small enough and dry enough to be burnt totally, leaving no ash or unconsumed material, will leave its negative impression as perfect in the mantle as will wax. I have cast the legs of grasshoppers into saws for ivory workers and cast real butterflies, wing perfect, by these means.

"And so I took the bees from the little box in which they had been brought. I killed each one with a needle . . . and I did so with as much reverential care as a priest would sacrifice seven bulls to Zeus. I mantled each fragile carapace and burnt it out of the mantle and, making each laborious insect laboriously immortal, I poured gold into these tiny molds. When, many hours later, I broke them open there were seven bees of solid gold. Each wing and every leg perfect, they lay on the palm of my hand.

"'Here in your honor, Artemis,' I said, 'the most fragile sacrifice ever made you. Each victim ritually killed, each pyre ritually kindled and behold, each is a votive to last forever.' And I fastened the bees upon the comb so that they seemed to be coming and going about their sacred business without which no man could cast the bronze doors of a temple to Apollo nor make any bronze sculpture."

In May, 1967, *The Maze Maker* was published in England. In January, 1968, George Wooller from New Zealand, who had read the book, asked me to make a golden honeycomb for him. "If," he said, "that is how it was done—do it!" It has been done, and we did it—not, I admit, in one attempt, for neither my friend John Donald, fine goldsmith though he is, nor I could rival Daedalus himself. We have, however, done it much as Daedalus described it, except that it was cast in a centrifuge and failed sixteen times before we achieved it because we lacked the weight of gold necessary to thrust its molten way through the walls of the comb, which were little more than the thickness of hairs. The bees, too, were cast by the method Daedalus describes, and when all was complete, the owner took it to New Zealand, where a friend, an apiarist, placed it among his hives to photograph it, and there real bees clustered upon it among their golden companions and began to come and go about their sacred business.

The "secret" of course, is simple. Metal has been cast by the lost-wax method for five thousand years, and a centrifuge can be contrived by whirling a vessel in circles on a string.*

In the fall of 1967 the book was published in America. A New York financier, Armand G. Erpf, read it and expressed interest in the maze itself. In effect, he too said, "If that is how it was done—do it," and it too is done. It

---

*For a more detailed description of this process, see "Unwearying Bronze," in the Winter, 1965, HORIZON.

In his book The Maze Maker *Ayrton credited Daedalus with having cast a golden honeycomb from a real one by means of the lost-wax process. Challenged to duplicate his protagonist's feat, Ayrton made this honeycomb (reproduced larger than actual size) after more than a dozen attempts.*

lies in a cup in the Catskill Mountains of New York, and it is built of stone and brick—210,000 bricks. It is two hundred feet across, with seven "decision points" spaced through it. At the center of its 1,680 feet of coil there are two chambers: one is inhabited by the Minotaur, the other by Daedalus himself, who is at work on the making of a maze, and his winged son, who leaps upward to fly out from the center into the sky.

As for me, I cloak myself for the time being in the last paragraphs of *The Maze Maker*, for if I am not Daedalus, perhaps I may quote him to illustrate on an epic scale what I suppose in smaller measure my own condition to be.

"I have called myself Maze Maker with a certain irony because although I believe myself pre-eminent in many crafts, I have been, as Minos described me, first and last a maker of labyrinths.

"All this long burrowing and building, to protect or to imprison, this flight through the sky and tunneling in the earth, seems to me now to add up to no more than the parts of a single great maze which is my life. This maze for the Maze Maker I made from experience and from circumstance. Its shape identifies me. It has been my goal and my sanctuary, my journey and its destination. In it I have lived continually, ceaselessly enlarging it and turning it to and fro from ambition, hope, and fear. Toy, trial, and torment, the topology of my labyrinth remains ambiguous. Its materials are at once dense, impenetrable, translucent, and illusory. Such a total maze each man makes round himself and each is different from every other, for each contains the length, breadth, height, and depth of his own life.

"I, Daedalus, maze maker, shall take this that I have written with me to Sardinia and dedicate it at the entrance to the maze which leads to death. Then you, before you follow me down into Gaia, who is the Mother, will know what is to be known of my journey and the fate of my son, Icarus. Before you follow me, look into the sky-maze and acknowledge Apollo who is the god."

London-born Michael Ayrton, although best known as a painter and sculptor, is a man of many parts. At one time or another he has been a poet, critic, novelist, film maker, broadcaster, and set designer.

65

The Mad World of Hieronymus Bosch

No painting in the history of art has so puzzled viewers as The Garden of Earthly Delights. *Only now, perhaps, in the godless, hedonist light of the twentieth century does its meaning become clear. For a new age of folly, a perceptive critic here interprets Bosch's blood-chilling message*

By GILBERT HIGHET

t hangs in the Prado Gallery in Madrid: one of the most enigmatic pictures ever painted. A couple of years ago I visited the Prado every day for a month. I always spent an hour or so studying this picture, trying to pierce through its layers of meaning, and I saw that it had a masterful effect upon every visitor. Beefy Germans, sweaty French, hairy and sandaled Americans, alert Japanese, all stopped dead in their tracks the moment they came upon it. Some, after a second glance of horror and bewilderment, turned abruptly away. Others stared at it in amazement, consulted their catalogues, and surveyed it slowly, shaking their heads. Others accepted its challenge; they stood back for a general overlook (it is a big painting) and then bent closer to investigate its curious details. Those who looked longest at it always walked away thoughtfully and gravely, glancing back occasionally as though trying to deepen the imprint the picture had made upon their minds. They might not comprehend it, but they would never forget it.

The painter is Hieronymus Bosch, who worked in 's Hertogenbosch in southern Holland from about 1480 to 1515 or so. He gave his picture no title whatever, and in some ways it is unlike any other paintings by Bosch himself or by other artists. It is unique—which means that its puzzles are that much harder to solve.

In shape it is rather complex. Most paintings are simple oblongs. This is a triptych, three paintings fastened together horizontally by hinges. And here is the first problem: the three pictures seem to have little or nothing to do with one another. They are different in theme, emotional tone, and composition. We might even suspect that they were really three separate paintings that some cautious owner had fixed together for safety. But Bosch himself indicated clearly that the three form a unit. The two side pictures fold together like shutters to cover the central panel; and on their backs Bosch has

painted a fourth scene, a unitary composition spreading over both and joining them inseparably. (Quite a number of altarpieces are arranged like this. Often they were kept shut during the week to protect the paintings within and to increase their impact on the congregation when they were thrown open on Sundays and holidays. But Bosch's work is not an altarpiece.) Looking at this complex arrangement and studying the scene painted on the backs of the side panels, we cannot help but conclude that Bosch intended us to see not three paintings but four, and to look at them in sequence: first, the scene on the outside as an introductory statement; and then, after the triptych is opened, the three inside, which come as a revelation.

(1)

On the back, that is, on the outer covering, Bosch has depicted a majestic scene glorifying the power of God the Creator. It shows the world on the third day of Creation, before mankind and the animals were called into existence (Genesis 1:9–13). The earth is there, and the sea surrounding it, and the clouds (stormy clouds) in the firmament above, and grass, and trees—some of them fantastic and to our eyes unnatural in shape. God sits far apart from the world, gazing at it and holding an open book (detail **1**). There is deep meaning in this. One of the great philosophical problems with which men have grappled, both before and after the establishment of Christianity, is (to put it bluntly) *why* the world ex-

ists with all its imperfections and mutabilities; *why* God created it, since God is from all eternity self-sufficient and does not need to produce a world of temporal change such as ours. You see the dilemma. Before the world was brought into being, God was perfect and infinite. What good did it do him to create it? He did not require worshipers; he did not need to demonstrate his power. He gained nothing by calling the world into existence, and would not suffer loss if he chose to blot it out into primal nothingness. Something of this mystery can be seen in the outer panels of Bosch's triptych: the earth appearing like a newborn planet; and God, although contemplating it and willing its existence, far removed from it and high above. In order to unite the two parts of this picture still more ineluctably, Bosch has written (in the tall, stiff Gothic script that appears elsewhere in his work) a bimembral sentence from the Book of Psalms:

For he spoke, and it was done; he commanded, and it stood fast.

Now let the triptych be opened. Three strange scenes appear. Only one is intelligible at first sight, and even that is full of quirks and oddities. The panel on the left shows a dreamlike garden. In the foreground is a divine figure, whose face and head, beard and robes, do not resemble those of God the Father, but rather those of Jesus as Bosch has depicted him elsewhere. He stands between two naked figures: Adam, just awakened from the sleep during which Eve was made out of his rib, and Eve, half-kneeling as though rising to her human stature for the first time. (This is the second, and more graphic, of the Bible's two accounts of the Creation of mankind, Genesis 2:21–25.) With his left hand God the Son holds the right wrist of Eve; he is at once giving her life and raising her from the ground and presenting her to Adam, who gazes at her with admiration. God the Son does not look at either of his creatures, but fixes his gaze directly upon us, the onlookers, raising his right hand in a gesture that certainly blesses the union of the couple and may also be extended to us.

So far the picture is clear, if slightly unorthodox. Other painters (and even Bosch himself), depicting the creation of Eve, make her actually rise out of the rib cage of the anesthetized Adam and show her being brought to life by God the Father, who is wearing a great crown like that of the Holy Roman Emperor. Nevertheless, there is one important Christian concept identifying Jesus with the Logos, the Word of God, which actually accomplished the work of creation. It appears in Milton's *Paradise Lost:*

> So spake the Almighty; and to
>   what he spake
> His Word, the Filial Godhead,
>   gave effect.

A thoughtful man like Hieronymus Bosch might portray God the Father as creating the world, and God the Son (who was to be incarnated) as creating one or both of the first human beings.

The scene is Paradise, the garden called Eden. Behind Adam is a peculiar tree, which must be the tree of knowledge of good and evil. Naturally it does not look like an ordinary fruit tree; its shape and habit are unique. Elsewhere in the garden are other trees and shrubs, some normal to our eyes, some dreamlike in form. From this we should not infer too much. Bosch knew that Paradise would not resemble an ordinary European garden, but would display the rich variety of God's creative imagination. He implicitly rejected the fashion, cultivated by many medieval painters, of making all the scenery in a Biblical picture perfectly recognizable and contemporary. Bosch in his religious paintings always interrupts the reality with fantasies, reminding us that his subjects are distant, exotic, or otherworldly. The bizarre rock-formations in his Paradise, and the grotesque fountain in its midst (4), are created by this belief. Remember also that the scenery and climate of the Low Countries tend to be flat, colorless, and mo-

notonous; Bosch made some of his paintings an escape from his homeland.

Yet when we look more closely, this landscape is not how we envisage the Garden of Eden. Although the world is newborn, and ought to be harmonious and peaceful, it already contains ugliness, cruelty, and something like madness. Beside the central fountain there is a rock formation that resembles a huge sleeping head: the mouth is made of a nasty, squirming snake, and there is a little swarm of disgusting reptiles at the neck (4). Furthermore, the orthodox belief is that before Adam's fall the animals lived at peace with one another:

> Sporting the lion ramped, and in
>   his paw
> Dandled the kid.

Not so here. Right in the foreground, where we cannot miss them, a cat has caught a mouse (2) and a fantastic bird is swallowing a live frog (3). In the rear a boar is threatening a lizard, which is snarling defiance. Even in Paradise, something is wrong.

The panel on the right, balancing Paradise, is hell. It is not the conventional medieval hell, where apelike devils torment sinners with instruments used by human torturers—pincers, hot irons, boiling oil. Nor is it an organized hell like that of Dante, which is the work of Divine Reason, constructed according to the three Aristotelian categories of wrongdoing: Incontinence, Violence, and Malice. It is

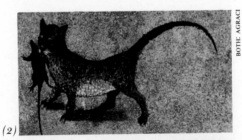

(2)

(3)

all like a drug dream, a nightmare, or the interior of a maniac's mind. This is one of the ruling ideas of Hieronymus Bosch: that health, virtue, and heaven are calm, orderly, and reasonable, while illness, sin, and hell are wild, random, and senseless. Besides Dante's Inferno, there are many other visions of hell that have been described in considerable detail by men of the Middle Ages. One is the Vision of Tundal, an Irishman whose guardian angel conducted him through the abode of the damned, allowing him to suffer many of its torments before returning him to life and repentance. But in all such descriptions I have read, hell is basically logical and systematic. It is a kingdom. Its citizens are the devils, who oppress the damned souls as the bad noblemen and their soldiers oppressed the peasants in earthly life. Its monarch, Satan, supernaturally huge and infernally hideous, reigns at its center, eternally tormented by God's decree, and himself tormenting the worst of human sinners, chewing and mangling them. In such a hell the fiends all do what bad human beings would do if they had almost infinite power and ingenuity. They appear to be using their minds to inflict pain; they are jailers, interrogators, torturers, working under a system of law and giving evil for evil. But for Bosch hell is the abrogation of the intellect. In his hell very little happens for any intelligible reason—except that sometimes a sinner is apparently punished by the worldly device that led him into sin, as when a soul who loved profane music too well is crucified on a harp, or when gamblers are pinned to the gaming table. But the monarch of Bosch's hell is not an angel in reverse, turned black and equipped with bat wings, nor, like Dante's Satan, a three-headed antithesis to the Holy Trinity. It is a monster in which nothing is human but the face, and that is not evil but almost vacuous (12). Its legs are dead trees, hollow and stripped of bark; its feet are ships in water, one nearly capsizing. Its body is a thin, empty eggshell

(4) Detail from left panel

"The Temptation of Saint Anthony"

inhabited by a few unconcerned figures and one beast. Its head is not a skull with a crown, but a flat disk surmounted by a bagpipe, around which little monsters (not very scary) lead sinners.

A subaltern demon (5) is punishing gluttons, which we can tell because he wears a cooking pot for a crown and beer jugs for shoes. He eats his victims alive and then excretes them into an open latrine. This is painful and disgusting; but it is also ridiculous—even, in a gruesome way, funny. Bosch makes it funnier by adding a silly-looking man to vomit into the mess and—anticipating Freud's identification of avarice with the childish collection of feces—by making a sinner void gold pieces into it from his anus. Some scholars suggest that this demon is Satan, ruler of the realm of hell—apparently because he sits on a perverted throne (a latrine seat) and occupies the foreground of the picture. But, although disgusting, he is neither large nor formidable, and he is avenging only one particular sin. He is not the monarch, for the monarch is the central monster. The one follower of Bosch who understood him best also

placed a fragile impotent being like Bosch's Tree-Demon at the central regnal point of hell: Pieter Bruegel, in *Dulle Griet*. Bosch means that Satan, after his fall, lost nearly all his godlike semblance and all his power; only the subordinate demons remain active. (A similar conception appears in Dante, where Lucifer, although enormous in bulk, is immobilized, stuck fast in the center of the earth and surrounded by eternal ice. He cannot move; he can only chew the three cardinal sinners and weep from his three pairs of eyes. But the minor fiends—Scarmiglione, Draghignazzo, Rubicante—move about actively, torturing sinners of lesser magnitude.

Whenever he deals with hell and the devils, Bosch repeats this master idea with many variations: the idea that they are illogical, disorderly, incomprehensible, crazy. When we hear that Saint Anthony was tempted in the desert, we expect that Bosch will depict the devils as the saint himself saw them, in the forms of beautiful women, disputatious spirits, helpful monks bringing meals, or dangerous armed men and wild beasts. Not so. Most of the figures surrounding Anthony and dis-

tracting him from prayer—even from a vision of the Saviour himself—are grotesque confusions of human, animal, and vegetable life mixed up with man-made objects. There is a hunchbacked dwarf on skates; he has a birdlike head capped by a funnel with a dead twig stuck in it. There is a fish, whose body is a fishing boat and who wears a cuirass and a dagger. There is a giant rat carrying a fish-tailed treeman holding a baby. There is a dogfaced unicorn with wings, no body, and a pair of *hind* legs. (He is constructed on the same plan as the little monster beside the giraffe in Paradise.) And the upper air is inhabited by flying fish, birdlike ships, and other defiances of the laws of reason and nature.

The forces of hell in this picture do not concentrate on carnal lust. They are not (like Mephistopheles) endeavoring chiefly to arouse their victim's passions by offering him savory food and rich wines and lovely girls. They are attempting to convince him that the world is quite meaningless, that there is no order in nature, that there is no reason why anything should be precisely what it is, that anything can come out of anything, that creation is

71

(5) Detail from right panel

being uncreated by the forces of unreason, and therefore that God is powerless or nonexistent. If you study the monstrosities in Bosch's paintings, you come to see that he intends them not to be static but to be constantly changing. Bosch suggests that most of the sufferings of Anthony under temptation were caused by the fact that things, as he looked at them, lost their shape and kept turning into something else and then into something else again. It is often ridiculous, this world of chaos, and sometimes quite comical. (There is a humorous charm in the distracted little bodiless head sailing along in a dinghy and being pecked at by a featherless flamingo.) But if you view God as the supreme power of Reason, if you wish to live in a universe of order, if you value your sanity more than your physical well-being, then such a vision is absolutely terrifying. Bosch himself must often have been tormented in the same way. When he looked at a growing tree during periods of doubt, he discerned a hideous face in its bark and its roots turned into twisting claws; a hollow trunk had something inside it, glaring out. When he saw a beer pot, it changed into an animal's body voiding liquid. His own house might have eyes for windows, and its door might seem like a greedy mouth gaping for a victim. A bagpipe was a bulging face with fat cheeks and a long nose. Even a broken eggshell was sinister, if only because it was so imperfect and frail and useless, and yet continued to exist.

And still there is something reassuring about Bosch's view of hell. It is insanity, but it is not rational, deliberate, ingenious cruelty. There are some scenes of physical suffering. Naked souls are pierced and sliced, transfixed and held in loathsome positions, terrified by monsters. But the cruelest of all tortures, the torture by fire promised in the Bible, is seldom shown—although Dante put the homosexuals on burning sand under a rain of flames, and the instruments of fiery torture devised by men in China and in medieval Europe for the infliction of pain on their fellow human beings make all Bosch's devils look like amateurs.

With this in mind, let us examine the big central panel in the triptych, standing between Paradise and hell. It is a vision: an unnatural landscape crowded with naked human figures, animals both real and surrealistic, grotesque conglomerations of bodies and vegetable shapes, and dreamlike fantasies. While I was last studying it in the Prado, a French couple came up and gazed at it for a few moments with increasing disapproval. After a couple of minutes the wife shrugged her shoulders, the husband said "*Insensé!*" and they walked out. The French believe that they are the chosen people of the Goddess of Reason—to whose honor they once rededicated the Cathedral of Notre Dame—and would naturally despise such a mess as this. (There are very few visionary painters in the history of French art: Gustave Moreau's mystical pictures are thin and vague, and there are only one or two notable French surrealist painters.)

But the couple were right, too. It is a picture of madness, of insensate folly. Virtually nobody is doing any of the things that men and women do in normal life; most of the huge crowd is very busy doing things that are absurd. The little group that best typifies the whole thing is composed of two people, stark naked, dancing merrily, interlocked by branches of a fruit tree, and wearing as a headdress a huge solemn owl (6). Others are standing in swimming pools (one of them head downward); some are playing with gigantic birds and fishes (8); many are riding animals, real and imaginary; many are just chatting or playing little tricks on one another; one is cuddling, not a girl, but a giant strawberry. Yet the remarkable thing is this: no one is doing anything really evil, and no one looks as if he or she were conceived and presented as positively wicked, dangerously sinful. The faces are mostly calm and composed. Everybody is about twenty years old. There are no old sinners or young perverts. No one is leering or slobbering with greed; no one is angry or overexcited. And although there are scores of men and women in the picture, all naked, few of them show any signs of sexual desire. One fellow standing in the river has grabbed a woman, who looks a bit shocked, as though such a thing were against the rules, and yet is returning his caress (8); another couple sitting inside a transparent bubble are fondling each other gently (9); and a third are exchanging a kiss through an aperture in a monstrous fruit. For the rest, it might be a well-conducted nudist camp. Though the people are naked, they do not appear sexy. (There is hardly any pubic hair visible.) One girl painted by Rubens, his second wife, Helena Fourment, has more sexual charge than all the naked women in the Bosch phantasmagoria; and in Bernini's statue of a couple, Pluto carrying off Persephone, there is a hundred times more lust than among all these tranquil nudes. And there is no violence worth mentioning. No one is robbing his neighbor, or torturing him, or trying to kill him. One character is sticking flowers into a friend's backside, but the friend looks as if he were enjoying it.

Now, what is the meaning of all this? The picture is often called "The Garden of Earthly Delights," but the occupations of its inhabitants are not the normal pleasures of humanity. It may be delightful to carry a six-foot-long mullet while riding a lion (7), but most of us can do without the experience. Hugging a huge strawberry, toting a large mussel shell with people inside it, and crowding into a big empty egg are occupations that give little enjoyment

(7)

73

and must soon grow boring.

As far as I can see, there are only two ways to understand the painting. One is to assume that it is filled with ethical meanings that are hidden behind symbolic acts and objects. In normal religious paintings nearly every detail may be a symbol. When the baby Jesus holds a goldfinch, for example, this is not only because children like to play with pet birds but also because the goldfinch was believed to love thorn-bushes and thus recalls the crown of thorns. The European blackbird sings beautifully, but looks sinister in his black costume, so he is a symbol of devilish temptation. In this picture, then, the big central group of men and women riding animals may be a symbolic presentation of sinners carried away by the deadly sins. Yet they do not fit the established conventions. The man on the lion is no doubt one of the Angry. But why is he carrying an enormous fish? There are two people on a camel; now the camel, because it can go so long without drinking, is a symbol of Temperance, but the riders are trying to tickle its neck and do not appear to typify self-control, or its opposite (**10**). So again, in Christian iconography the strawberry symbolizes perfect virtue because it is all sweet fruit without a stone and because it is so humble, hiding itself on the ground under leaves (the Virgin Mary sometimes has her robe embroidered with strawberries). Why are several of these naked people—among whom not a single sign of the Christian faith is to be seen—caressing large strawberries with expressions of appetite? Raspberries also appear, and imaginary fruits that have never existed in this world and so cannot be general sym-

bols. Many of Bosch's creations appear nowhere else in the universe of medieval imagery. Apparently it is impossible to bring all the dream-objects of this picture into a single pattern governed by any well-known and acknowledged type of symbolism and to say that, when interpreted thus, they form a coherent description of some aspect of human life.

A variant of this explanation has been advanced. This is that the painting is a difficult message in cipher: that it is a sermon for a few chosen people, concealed by a set of esoteric symbols that were never widely known and are now all but forgotten. The symbols (we are told) were used by a group that practiced a secret religion, not Christian, which was therefore heretical and subject upon discovery to terrible punishments, but which considered itself nobler and purer and more enlightened than Christianity with its laxities and abuses. This is certainly possible. How many moderns have ever heard of the heretical sect called the Cathari, the Pure People? Yet its members were powerful in northern Italy and southern France for at least a hundred years, and it took a crusade to stamp them out. There were other such sects, all underground, using apocalyptic symbols and rituals. Some of them were Adamite and believed in collective nudity at their gatherings. It has therefore been suggested that this painting shows a meeting of such a group, idealized as a heaven of physical and spiritual harmony, and that the many strange animals and objects are, or represent, parts of the ritual of the sect.

This I find impossible to believe. Many of the things that the people are doing are so silly, so obviously meant to be contemptible in a light, childish way, that we cannot be intended to respect them as enlightened characters who have a secret insight into the ultimate meaning of life. There is no sign of God or godliness. No religious feeling appears in even the smallest detail; the people live for themselves and one

another in a brittle, dreamlike present, without effort, aspiration, or ideal.

In centuries before our own time this central picture must have appeared wildly remote from actual life. It was obscenity, or it was mania. Today, however, it is not so far removed from our experience. A crowd of naked people stands and sits around, while others ride aimlessly in circles with no destination in sight, and still others swim languidly, or dive, or do gymnastics beside the water. There are birds, flowers, fruits. The girls' hair falls straight down their bare shoulders with only a hint of a wave (**11**). A few black men and women mingle with the white groups, peacefully accepted. The landscape is a phantasmagoria. Does not the whole thing look like a colony of flower people in a collective happening? The innocent, unlined, vacuous faces, the bland joy in unanimous nudity, the silly little games with fruit, and above all, the lack of purpose and direction and will power, the absolute denial of any goal in life except the simplest pleasures of immediate existence and untrammeled movement and indiscriminate gregariousness—does not the whole painting portray the life of the young in many countries today?

Then what do the strange objects and animals signify? Do they mean anything at all? Charles de Tolnay, whose magnificent book *Hieronymus*

(10)

(9) Detail from central panel

(11)

Bosch is essential for all students of the master painter, thinks many are the sexual symbols that people have long known but that Freud was the first to bring within the sphere of intellectual analysis: apples = breasts, and so forth. Yet many simple objects appear to have different and even conflicting meanings. D. Bax (quoted by de Tolnay) proposes that a bagpipe is an allusion to the female sex organ. But look at the taut bag with the stiff, erect drone protruding from it: is that female or male? Some of these images are sexual; many are not, or are not clearly so. Perhaps, then, they are ethical and belong to Flemish folklore, are visual proverbs, in fact. If so, a bagpipe need be neither male nor female. It can be a symbol of vanity and wasted effort: a bag of wind requiring great effort to produce poor, cheap, simple-minded music. Much of the Flemish folklore of five hundred years ago has disappeared. Here and there we can recognize an obvious symbol: the glass bubble, the broken eggshell, the bundle of hay. But if we stand back and look at this picture, or at any of Bosch's fantasies (as distinct from his realistic paintings that show the sufferings of Jesus or his straightforward illustrations of the seven deadly sins), we shall be compelled to conclude that he intended to puzzle us, to bewilder us, to show us a vision that is as vivid as real life but as irrational as a long-lasting nightmare.

Apart from the individual images, so many of them incomprehensible, what is the meaning of the whole central picture? What is its significance as the center of the triptych?

The most notable fact about it is that there is no religion in the entire scene. Bosch was working about 1510, when most of western Europe was Christian and Catholic. Everywhere you looked, there was a church or a wayside shrine, a cross or a saint's statue. The calendar was arranged around the festivals of the Christian religion. The greatest and oldest monarchy in the West was controlled by the pope, the Vicar of Christ. Every land was full of communities of monks and nuns, often owning large properties. The laws of the Church competed with, and sometimes dominated, the laws of secular communities. The very air was filled with the sound of church bells regulating human life. But in the world portrayed here there is no religion, neither cross nor altar, neither priest nor parishioner, and, shall we say, neither saint nor sinner? It is like a dream of a pagan world, silly, simple, free.

Then why is it placed in the center of this trio of paintings, with Paradise on one side and hell on the other? What do the three conjoined paintings mean?

No one knows. All solutions to the question are more or less educated guesses. This is only one more guess. It will not be simple, because Bosch's paintings cannot have been executed to convey one simple message; but it will be clear in outline.

Humanity is going to hell. We are all doomed, all damned.

Secondly. We are not vicious, wicked, repulsive criminals. We are fools. Sin is folly.

Thirdly. The mission of Jesus Christ was perfectly useless. At the very moment when the human and animal world was created, cruelty and sin were part of Paradise. The naked society has never heard of the Incarnation and the Crucifixion, it does not know that mankind fell with the sin of Adam, it does not believe that Jesus came to the earth to redeem us, it would rather stand in swimming pools and ride griffins than think about repentance and virtue and heaven and hell. It is a world without Christ and without religion.

Mankind therefore lives in a home for the insane, which—like drugtakers and their suppliers today—it has built and equipped for itself. It is ruining its intellect and its power of self-direction. In the end it will hand itself over to the powers of darkness and madness. Eternity will be a lunatic asylum.

This is a message of desperate pessimism. Even the darkest of the Christian books in the Bible, the Book of Revelation, draws to its end with a battle waged by the Incarnate Word of God against the monstrous beast, the false prophet, and their followers. Then comes the Last Judgment, and after that the radiant vision of the Heavenly City, the New Jerusalem, gleaming forever with the splendor of the Lord God shed upon his servants. Hell exists for the damned; but some souls are saved, and for them there is a promise of eternal life. Not so in the vision of Bosch, which moves through universal folly to endless damnation, without a hope of heaven.

Another of his triptychs, called *The Hay-Wain,* almost equally complex, carries a similar message. On the backs of the side panels, which can be closed to cover it, there is a single picture, brilliantly painted but bitter and sad: a poor, elderly, homeless peddler defending himself with a stick against a snarling dog (*The Hay-Wain:* front panel). In the background on one side a couple are dancing to a shepherd's bagpipe; on the other, a traveler is being robbed and stripped and tied to a tree. In the distance there are a gibbet and a torture wheel; in the foreground, the skull and leg bone of a horse, with two carrion crows. The peddler—who is he? Is

"The Hay-Wain": front panel

MUSEO DEL PRADO

"The Hay-Wain"

he the type of the virtuous soul, exiled and wandering through an alien world? Might his face be a self-portrait of Hieronymus Bosch?

Inside, this triptych is arranged in much the same way as the other: on the left, the Garden of Eden; on the right, hell; and in the center, a symbolic picture of human folly and sin. The depiction of Paradise is complicated. Reading downward from top to bottom, it shows four scenes in a time-sequence: first, God in heaven contemplating the fall of the rebellious angels, who are being transformed into hideous insectiform monsters; then, God the Father creating Eve; next, the serpent tempting Eve; last, the expulsion of our first parents after they commit the first human sin. God's own angels revolted against him; God's first human creatures broke his commandment.

Hell, on the right, is (as in the other triptych) surrounded by an atmosphere of smoke and flames and inhabited by strange demoniac beings, part or wholly animal in form. A few naked human souls are undergoing torture and being conducted or driven from left to right, farther into hell. In the middle devils are busily building a strong tower—so that, when we glance from left to right, we see God's world failing and the world of the fiends succeeding and being strengthened.

The large central panel shows a procession moving toward the right—that is, away from Paradise and toward hell. It contains many types of human beings, but it is led by demons. There are the Holy Roman Emperor, the pope, a scepter-bearing king or prince, and other grave and important personalities. Before these dignitaries is a huge wagon piled with hay. Hay is worthless except as fodder for animals. Therefore this must mean that the pursuits of human life are worthless, materialistic, cheap. Furthermore, the Bible compares human life to grass, which grows up and (in Biblical lands) dies quickly. Men are "like grass which groweth up. In the morning it flourisheth, and groweth up; in the evening it is cut down, and withereth." Some scholars have added another interpretation. They suggest that Bosch is picturing a Flemish proverb, rather like the one that Byron put into an epigram:

> The world is a bundle of hay,
> Mankind are the asses who pull;
> Each tugs it a different way,
> And the greatest of all is John Bull.

And indeed, several people are grabbing for hunks of hay from the wagon. One man has fallen off his ladder still clutching his parcel, and two people are fighting over a sheaf. The top of the hay load is occupied by two pairs of lovers, one pair smooching, the other playing and singing. A dancing devil accompanies the music. A kneeling angel prays for help, gazing up to heaven, where God the Son appears—but is seen by none except the angel.

The groups of people surrounding the hay wagon typify various kinds of silliness and wrongdoing. A woman quarreling with a cripple is about to knife him. A duelist has disarmed his opponent and is cutting his throat. A fat friar is drinking in a bemused way and ignoring a nun who is praying for him. The wagon itself is moving very slowly—or has stopped, since two men are mixed up with the wheels. But it is going to move. Although we do not see who or what is pulling it, it is preceded by a gang of devils all marching purposefully rightward toward hell: snarling cat-faced, stag-headed, fish-bodied, beaked, and furred like beings in a nightmare, they stride purposefully onward with an air of confidence and even triumph. Three of them are holding something that may be one of the shafts of the hay wagon; if it is, they are supplying the motive power. Look at their energy. Look at the zest with which they move. They are victorious. They are taking over. Look at the calm impercipient faces of the great men following in this triumphal procession; they are satisfied with their movement through the world and do not know where it is leading them. Lastly, look at Christ in the heavens above, at his gesture. That is not the orderly sign of blessing. The Saviour has thrown up his arms, to indicate helplessness. The original creation of angels and mankind went wrong, and the act of redemption through his sacrifice on the cross has proved to be useless. Mankind, in spite of God, is determined to go to hell.

Both *The Hay-Wain* and *The Garden of Earthly Delights* are triptychs of a rather uncommon type. When an artist executes three paintings, one large picture and two flanking panels, he naturally concentrates attention on the central scene. But he usually makes the other two face inward to that scene. For instance, the central panel will show the Nativity, with the infant Jesus, and Mary, and Joseph. On the left appear the Wise Men of the East; on the right, the shepherds; all are gazing at the baby. But in these paintings by Hieronymus Bosch, although the intellectual emphasis remains on the center panel, the eye is meant to move

from left to right, both in space and in time: from creation and Paradise long ago, through the present scene of ephemeral folly, to the infinite future in hell. Van Eyck shows eternity touching time in one glorious moment. Bosch shows the history of mankind as a long fool's errand leading inexorably to disaster.

This, then, is the meaning of both triptychs. Strictly speaking, they are blasphemous and heretical. It is not heretical to portray a boozy friar or a foolish pope. It *is* heretical to declare that the Incarnation of God was in vain, that Jesus did not succeed in redeeming humanity, that there is no hope of heaven, no reward for virtue, no divine grace bestowed on even a small part of mankind, and that, whatever we all do or try to do, we are traveling the primrose path to the everlasting bonfire. It is a concept hard for all but the bitterest pessimist to accept.

For another reason it is difficult to understand this message of Bosch. This is that he views sin very much as though it were merely folly. When you and I contemplate human wickedness, we think first of cruelty and killing—the Nazi death-camps, the Japanese atrocities committed against prisoners of war, the crimes that defile our cities. And then we think of other crimes, which do not destroy at once, but which corrupt: the huge wealthy organizations manufacturing and peddling mind-destroying drugs and filthy books to pervert immature souls. And then—but why go on? We are surrounded, harassed, haunted, by man's inhumanity to man. Sometimes in dreams I see decent people as a group of pilgrims (like Bosch's peddler) looking for a better place, a safer, cleaner place to live, but attacked and plagued by the devils of this world, human in face and animal in soul. The quiet rabbi brutalized by the concentration-camp guard, the helpless American or Australian soldier beaten and vilified by the Japanese sergeant, each viewed his tormentors as fiends who were scarcely

human by any definition. But this aspect of man's wickedness Bosch hardly sees. His admirer and successor Pieter Bruegel knew it well. Bruegel lived when the Spaniards were oppressing the Netherlands with fire and sword, and so he painted *The Massacre of the Innocents* (where the victims are Dutch families, and the tyrants Spanish soldiery) and other scenes of strife and slaughter. Hieronymus Bosch, however, considers that sin should be regarded as mere foolishness. He seldom envisages the darker aspects of sin. On earth he will show a few men fighting or stealing; intensive cruelty and torture (apart from the sufferings of Jesus) he places not in this world but in hell. This is because he lived and worked in a world that was, although profoundly corrupt in his sight, comparatively peaceful. There were civil disorders in the Netherlands during his lifetime, but they were not seriously destructive; and the cities were growing in prosperity (Antwerp being the richest seaport in Europe after Venice). What Bosch saw around him was a fat and flourishing world in which the body was hypertrophied and the spirit decaying. It was in his era that a German thinker, Sebastian Brant, wrote one of the most famous late-medieval satires, *Ship of Fools*, which showed all sorts and conditions of men as idiots bound for the land of Stupidity—a concept that Bosch himself illustrated in an early picture. About the very time that Bosch was at work on this fantastic vision, Erasmus produced an immortal ironic encomium of Folly, the deity who really, above everything else, rules mankind. The greatest paintings of Hieronymus Bosch are inspired by that spirit of bitter laughter and comtemptuous despair.

Gilbert Highet is Anthon Professor of the Latin Language at Columbia University and Chairman of HORIZON's *Advisory Board. A long-time devotee of artistic riddles, he unraveled a Bruegel painting for the Spring, 1967, issue of* HORIZON: *"Where is the Bridegroom?"*

(12) This detail shows the face of the monarch of hell at the center of the right-hand panel.

FUTURE SHOCK

Eons ago the shrinking seas cast millions of unwilling aquatic creatures onto the newly created beaches. Deprived of their familiar environment, they died, gasping and clawing for each additional instant of eternity. Only a fortunate few better suited to amphibian existence survived the shock of change. Today, says the sociologist Lawrence Suhm of the University of Wisconsin, "We are going through a period as traumatic as the evolution of man's predecessors from sea creatures to land creatures . . . Those who can adapt will; those who can't will either go on surviving somehow at a lower level of development or will perish—washed up on the shores."

To assert that man must adapt seems superfluous. He has already shown himself to be among the most adaptable of life forms. He has survived equatorial summers and arctic winters. He has survived Dachau and Vorkuta. He has walked the lunar surface. Such accomplishments give rise to the glib notion that his adaptive capabilities are "infinite" or "boundless." Yet nothing could be further from the truth. For despite all his stamina, man remains a biological organism, a "biosystem," and all such systems operate within inexorable limits.

Temperature, pressure, caloric intake, oxygen and carbon-dioxide levels, all set absolute boundaries beyond which man, as presently constituted, cannot venture. Thus when we hurl a man into outer space, we surround him with an exquisitely designed microenvironment that maintains all these factors within livable limits. How strange, therefore, that when we hurl a man into the future, we take few pains to protect him from the shock of change. It is as though NASA had shot Armstrong naked into the cosmos.

In 1965, in an article in HORIZON magazine, I coined the term "future shock" to suggest the dizzying disorientation and the breakdown of rational response that occur when people are overwhelmed by demands for rapid adaptation.* Different individuals react to future shock in different ways. Its symptoms also vary according to the stage and intensity of the disease. These symptoms range all the way from anxiety, hostility to helpful authority, and seemingly senseless violence, to physical illness, depression, and apathy. Its victims often manifest

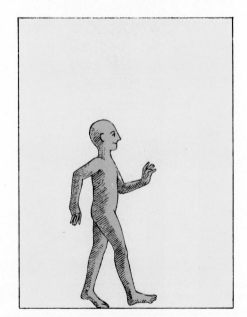

erratic swings in interest and life style, followed by an effort to "crawl into their shells" through social, intellectual, and emotional withdrawal. They feel continually harassed or tormented and want desperately to reduce the number of decisions they must make.

Noting the swift acceleration of change throughout the high-technology nations, I warned at the time that "the malaise, mass neurosis, irrationality, and free-floating violence already apparent in contemporary life" might be no more than a foretaste of tomorrow unless we came to understand—and prevent—future shock.

Since then, research in medicine, psychiatry, neurology, experimental psychology, and communications theory has lent credence to this warning. At the same time, the rate of change itself has skyrocketed. Furthermore, it has become clear that rising levels of novelty and diversity in the environment are compounding the intense adaptive difficulties inherent in the accelerative thrust. In short we are creating an environment so filled with astonishments, twists, reversals, eruptions, mind-jangling crises, and innovations as to test the limits of man's adaptive capability. We are setting the stage for future shock on a vast scale. In so doing we are threatening the future of rationality itself.

This is not the place to describe the physical distress produced by future shock—the illnesses that break out in a population after it has been subjected to extremely rapid rates of

*See "The Future as a Way of Life," Summer, 1965.

By ALVIN TOFFLER

High-powered change may be the central fact of our time,

yet we know very little about its effects.

We may, our author warns, be racing toward the most devastating

outbreak of mass hysteria in history

change. Startling research conducted in the United States, Japan, and Europe has found a direct correlation between the amount of adaptation and change in the life of an individual and the amount and severity of subsequent illness. We are beginning to document the assertion of such scientific pioneers as Hans Selye and René Dubos that too much environmental change takes a heavy physical toll on the individual. Studies among a wide variety of groups, from unemployed blacks in Watts to naval officers at sea, from pregnant women and the families of leukemia victims to retirees and college athletes, have now established beyond serious question that "alterations in life style" that require a great deal of adjustment and coping correlate with sickness—whether or not these changes are under the individual's direct control, whether or not he views them as desirable. Furthermore, the higher degree of life change, the higher the risk that subsequent illness will be severe.

If future shock were a matter of physical illness alone, it might be easier to prevent and to treat. But future shock attacks the psyche as well. Just as the body cracks under the strain of environmental overstimulation, the "mind" and its decision processes behave erratically when overloaded. By indiscriminately racing the engines of change we may be undermining not merely the health of those least able to adapt but their very ability to act rationally on their own behalf.

The striking signs of confusional breakdown can be seen all around us. The spreading use of drugs, the rise of mysticism, the recurrent outbreaks of vandalism and undirected violence, the politics of nihilism and nostalgia, the sick apathy of millions—all can be understood better if we recognize their relationship to future shock. These forms of social irrationality may well reflect the deterioration of individual decision-making under conditions of environmental overstimulation.

Psychophysiologists studying the impact of change on various organisms have shown that successful adaptation can occur only when the level of stimulation—the amount of change and novelty in the environment—is neither too high nor too low. "The central nervous system of a higher animal," says Professor D. E. Berlyne of the

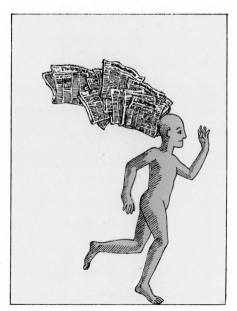

University of Toronto, "is designed to cope with environments that produce a certain rate of . . . stimulation . . . It will naturally not perform at its best in an environment that overstresses or overloads it." He makes the same point about environments that understimulate it. Indeed, experiments with deer, dogs, mice, and men all point unequivocally to the existence of what might be called an "adaptive range" below which and above which the individual's ability to cope simply falls apart.

Future shock is the response to overstimulation and occurs when the individual is forced to operate above his adaptive range. Considerable research has been devoted to determining the impact of inadequate change and novelty on human performance. Studies of men in isolated Antarctic outposts, experiments in sensory deprivation, investigations into on-the-job performance in factories, all show a falling off of mental and physical abilities in response to understimulation. We have less direct data on the impact of overstimulation, but such evidence as does exist is dramatic and unsettling.

Soldiers in battle often find themselves trapped in environments that are rapidly changing, unfamiliar, and unpredictable. To survive in such overstimulating environments, the soldier is driven to operate in the upper reaches of his adaptive range. Sometimes he is pushed beyond his limits.

During World War II a bearded Chindit soldier, fighting with General Wingate's forces behind the Japanese lines in Burma, actually fell asleep while a storm of machine-gun bullets splattered around him. Subsequent investigation revealed that this soldier was not merely reacting to physical fatigue or lack of sleep but surrendering to a sense of overpowering apathy.

Death-inviting lassitude was so common among guerrilla troops who had penetrated behind enemy lines that British military physicians gave it a name. They termed it Long Range Penetration Strain. This deadly lethargy, moreover, was not confined to guerrillas. A year after the Chindit incident similar symptoms cropped up en masse among the Allied troops who invaded Normandy, and British researchers, after studying five thousand combat casualties, concluded that this strange apathy was merely the final stage in a complex process of psychological collapse.

Mental deterioration often began with fatigue. This was followed by confusion and nervous irritability. The soldier became hypersensitive to the slightest stimuli. He would "hit the dirt" at the least provocation. He seemed unable to distinguish between the sound of enemy fire and other, less threatening sounds. He became tense, anxious, and irascible. His comrades never knew when he would respond violently to even minor inconvenience.

Then the final stage of emotional exhaustion set in. The soldier became, in the words of R. L. Swank, who headed the British investigation, "listless . . . mentally and physically retarded, preoccupied." Even his face became dull and apathetic. He gave up the struggle to save himself, to guide himself rationally through the battle. He seemed to lose the very will to live.

That men behave irrationally when thrown into conditions of high change and novelty is also borne out by studies of human behavior in times of fire, flood, earthquake, and other disasters. Even the most stable and "normal" people, unhurt physically, can be hurled into anti-adaptive states. Re-

duced to total confusion and mindlessness, they often seem incapable of the most elementary rational decision-making. Thus, in a study of the responses to tornadoes in Texas, H. E. Moore writes that "the first reaction . . . may be one of dazed bewilderment, sometimes one of disbelief, or at least refusal to accept the fact. This, it seems to us, is the essential explanation of the behavior of persons and groups in Waco when it was devastated in 1953 . . . On the personal level, it explains why a girl climbed into a music store through a broken display window, calmly purchased a record, and walked out again, even though the plate glass front of the building had been blown out and articles were flying through the air inside the building." The classic disaster photograph shows a mother holding a dead or wounded baby in her arms, her face blank and numb as though she could no longer comprehend the reality around her. Sometimes she sits rocking gently on her porch with a doll, instead of a baby, in her arms.

Culture shock, the profound disorientation suffered by the traveler who has plunged without adequate preparation into an alien culture, provides still another example of adaptational breakdown. Here we find none of the obvious elements of war or disaster. The scene may be totally peaceful and

safe. Yet the situation demands repeated adaptation to new and unexpected conditions.

The culture-shocked person, like the soldier and the disaster victim, is forced to grapple with unfamiliar and unpredictable events, relationships, and objects. His habitual ways of accomplishing things—even simple tasks like placing a telephone call—are no longer appropriate. The strange society may itself be changing only very slowly. Yet for him all is new. Signs, sounds, and other psychological cues rush past him before he can grasp their meaning. The entire experience takes on a surrealistic air. Every word, every action, is shot through with uncertainty. In this setting fatigue arrives more quickly than usual. Along with it the cross-cultural traveler often experiences what the psychologist Sven Lundstedt describes as "a subjective feeling of loss, and a sense of isolation and loneliness."

The unpredictability arising from novelty undermines his sense of reality. Thus he longs, as Professor Lundstedt puts it, "for an environment in which the gratification of important psychological and physical needs is predictable." He becomes "anxious, confused and often appears apathetic." Culture shock, Lundstedt concludes, may be seen as a "response to stress by emotional and intellectual withdrawal."

It is hard to read these (and many other) accounts of behavior breakdown under a variety of stresses without becoming acutely aware of their similarities. While there are differences, to be sure, between a soldier in combat, a disaster victim, and a culturally dislocated traveler, all three find themselves in circumstances involving rapid change, a high degree of novelty, or both. And all three respond to overstimulation first with confusion, then with anxiety and extreme irritability, and finally with apathy and emotional withdrawal. In short the available evidence strongly suggests that overstimulation may lead to bizarre and anti-adaptive behavior.

We still know too little about this

phenomenon to explain authoritatively why overstimulation seems to produce maladaptive behavior. But we do know that overstimulation can occur on at least three different levels: the sensory, the cognitive, and the decisional.

The easiest of these to understand is the sensory level. Just as sensory deprivation can lead to bewilderment and impaired mental functioning, so can the input of too much disorganized, patternless, or chaotic sensory stimuli have similar effects. The religious fervor and bizarre behavior of certain hippie cultists, for example, may arise not merely from drug abuse but from group experimentation with both sensory deprivation and sensory bombardment. The chanting of monotonous mantras, the attempt to focus the individual's attention upon interior bodily sensations to the exclusion of outside stimuli, are efforts to induce the weird and sometimes hallucinatory effects of understimulation.

At the other end of the scale we note the glazed stares and expressionless faces of young dancers at the great rock-music auditoriums where light shows, split-screen movies, high-decibel screams, shouts, and moans, grotesque costumes, and writhing, painted bodies create a sensory environment characterized by high input and extreme unpredictability and novelty.

An organism's ability to cope with sensory input is dependent upon its physiological structure. The nature of its sense organs and the speed with which impulses flow through its neural system set biological bounds on the quantity of sensory data it can accept. If we examine the speed of signal transmission within various organisms, we find that the lower the evolutionary level, the slower the movement. Thus, for example, in a sea-urchin egg, which lacks a nervous system as such, a signal moves along a membrane at a rate of about a centimeter an hour. Clearly, at such a rate, the organism can respond to only a very limited part of its environment.

Yet even in man, with a neural trans-mission rate of about thirty thousand centimeters per second, the limits of the system are imposing. (Electrical signals in a computer, by contrast, travel billions of times faster.) The limitations of the sense organs and the nervous system mean that many environmental events occur at rates too fast for us to follow, and we are reduced to sampling experience at best. When the signals reaching us are regular and repetitive, this sampling process can yield a fairly good mental representation of reality. But when it is highly disorganized, when it is novel and unpredictable, the accuracy of our imagery is necessarily reduced. Our image of reality is distorted. This may explain why, when we experience sensory overstimulation, we suffer confusion, a blurring of the line between illusion and reality.

If overstimulation at the sensory level increases the distortion with which we perceive reality, cognitive overstimulation interferes with our ability to "think." While some human responses to novelty are involuntary, others depend upon our ability to absorb, evaluate, and retain information.

Rational behavior in particular depends upon a ceaseless flow of data from the environment. It relies on the power of the individual to predict, with at least fair success, the outcome of his

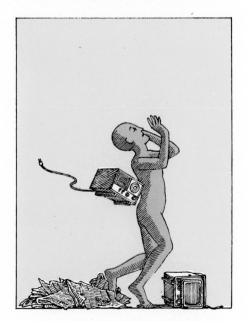

own actions. Sanity itself thus hinges on man's ability to predict his immediate, personal future on the basis of information fed him by the environment.

When the individual is plunged into a fast and irregularly changing situation or a novelty-loaded context, however, his predictive accuracy plummets. He can no longer make the reasonably correct assessments on which rational behavior is inevitably dependent.

To compensate for this, he must absorb far more information than before, and do it faster. Yet just as there are limits on how much sensory input we can accept, there are built-in constraints on our ability to process information. By classifying information, by abstracting and "coding" it in various ways, we manage to stretch these limits, but ample evidence demonstrates that our capabilities are finite.

Imagine, for example, an assembly-line worker in a factory that makes childrens' blocks. His job is to press a button each time a red block passes in front of him on the conveyor belt. As long as the belt moves at a reasonable speed, he will have little difficulty. We know, however, that if the pace is too slow, his mind will wander, and his performance will deteriorate. We also know that if the belt moves too fast, he will falter, miss, and grow confused. He is likely to become tense and irritable. He may take a swat at the machine out of frustration. Ultimately, he will give up trying to keep pace.

The information demands here are simple, but picture a more complex task. Now the blocks streaming down the line are of many different colors. The worker's instructions are to press the button only when a certain color pattern appears—a yellow block, say, followed by two reds and a green. In this task he must take in and process far more information before he can decide whether or not to hit the button. All other things being equal, he will have even greater difficulty keeping up as the pace of the line accelerates.

In a still more demanding task we not only force the worker to process a lot of data before deciding *whether* to hit the button, but we then force him to decide *which* of several buttons to press. Experiments like these have been built up to dismaying degrees of complexity. Tests have involved flashing lights, musical tones, letters, symbols, spoken words, and a wide array of other stimuli. And subjects, asked to drum finger tips, speak phrases, solve puzzles, and perform an assortment of other tasks, have been reduced to blithering ineptitude.

Clearly these findings can help us understand certain forms of psychological upset. Managers plagued by demands for rapid, incessant, and complex decisions; pupils deluged with facts and hit with repeated tests; housewives confronted with squalling children, jangling telephones, broken washing machines, the wail of rock 'n' roll from the teenager's room, and the whine of the television set in the den— may well find their ability to think and act impaired by the waves of information crashing into their senses. Is it not possible that some of the symptoms noted among battle-stressed soldiers, disaster victims, and culture-shocked travelers come from this kind of information overload?

Without fully understanding its potential impact, we are accelerating the generalized rate of change in society, compelling people to adapt to a new life pace, to confront novel situations and master them in ever shorter intervals. We are forcing them to choose among fast-multiplying options. We are, in other words, forcing them to process information at a far more rapid pace than was necessary in slowly evolving societies. There can be little doubt that we are subjecting at least some of them to cognitive overstimulation. What consequences this may have for mental health in the technosocieties has yet to be determined.

Whether or not we are submitting masses of men to information overload, we are affecting their behavior negatively by imposing on them still a third form of overstimulation—deci-

sion stress. Many individuals trapped in dull or slowly changing environments yearn to break out into new jobs or roles that will require them to make faster and more complex decisions. But among the people of the future the problem is reversed. "Decisions, decisions," they mutter as they race anxiously from task to task. The reason they feel harried is that transience and novelty and social diversity pose contradictory demands and thus place them in an excruciating double bind. The accelerative thrust forces us to quicken the tempo of private and public decision-making. New needs and novel crises demand rapid responses.

Yet the very newness of the circumstances brings about a revolutionary change in the nature of the decisions we are called upon to make. The rapid injection of novelty into the environment upsets the delicate balance of "programmed" and "nonprogrammed" decisions in our organizations and our private lives.

A programmed decision is one that is routine, repetitive, and easy to make. The commuter climbs aboard the 8:05, as he has done every day for years. Having long ago decided that the 8:05 is the most convenient run on the schedule, he boards the train almost out of reflex action. Because the immediate criteria on which the decision is based

are relatively simple and clear-cut, because all the circumstances are familiar, he scarcely has to think about it. He is required to process very little information. In this sense programmed decisions are low in psychic cost.

Contrast this with the kinds of decisions that same commuter thinks about on his way to the city. Should he take the new job Corporation X has just offered him? Should he buy a new house? Should he have an affair with his secretary? How can he get the management committee to accept his proposals about the new ad campaign? Such questions demand nonroutine answers. They force him to make one-time or first-time decisions that will establish new habits and behavorial procedures. Many factors must be studied and weighed. A vast amount of information must be processed. These decisions are nonprogrammed and are high in psychic cost.

For each of us life is a blend of the two. If this blend is too high in programmed decisions, we are not challenged; we find life boring and stultifying. We search, even unconsciously, for ways to introduce novelty into our lives, thereby altering the decision "mix." But if this mix is too high in nonprogrammed decisions, if we are hit by so many novel situations that programming becomes impossible, life comes to be painfully disorganized, exhausting, and anxiety-filled.

"There is no more miserable person," wrote William James, "than the one for whom the lighting of every cigar, the drinking of every cup . . . the beginning of every bit of work are subjects of deliberation." Unless we can extensively program our behavior, we waste tremendous amounts of information-processing capacity on trivial matters. Pushed to its extreme, the end-point is psychosis.

In a familiar context we are able to handle many of our life problems with low-cost programmed decisions. Change and novelty boost the psychic price of decision-making. When we move to a new neighborhood, for example, we are forced to alter old relationships and establish new routines or habits. Yet this cannot be done without first discarding thousands of formerly programmed decisions and making a whole series of costly first-time, nonprogrammed decisions. In effect we are asked to reprogram ourselves.

The same thing is true of the unprepared visitor to an alien culture, and it is equally true of the man who, still in his own society, is rocketed into the future without advance warning. The arrival of the future in the form of novelty and change makes all his painfully pieced-together behavioral routines obsolete. He suddenly discovers to his horror that these old routines, rather than solving his problems, merely intensify them. New and as yet unprogrammable decisions are demanded. In short, novelty disturbs the decision mix, tipping the balance toward the most difficult, most costly form of decision-making.

Some people, of course, can tolerate more novelty than others. The optimum mix is different for each of us. Yet the number and type of decisions demanded of us are not under our own control. It is the society that basically determines the mix of decisions we must make and the pace at which we must make them. Today there is a hidden conflict in our lives between the pressures of acceleration and those of novelty. One forces us to make faster decisions, while the other compels us to make more careful decisions.

The anxiety generated by this conflict is sharply intensified by expanding diversity. Increasing the choices open to an individual also increases the amount of information he needs to process if he is to deal with them.

It is the frontal collision of these incompatible demands that is now producing a decision-making crisis in the technosocieties. Taken together, these pressures justify the term decisional overstimulation, and they help explain why many men in these societies already feel themselves harried, futile, incapable of working out their private

futures. The conviction that the rat race is too tough, that things are out of control, is the inevitable consequence of these clashing forces. For the runaway acceleration of scientific, technological, and social change subverts the power of the individual to make sensible, competent decisions about his own destiny.

When we combine the effects of decisional stress with sensory and cognitive overload, we produce several common forms of individual maladaptation. One widespread response to high-speed change is outright denial. The Denier's strategy is to "block out" unwelcome reality. When the demand for decisions reaches a crescendo, he flatly refuses to take in new information. Like the disaster victim whose face registers total disbelief, the Denier cannot accept the evidence of his senses. Thus he concludes that things really are the same and that all evidence of change is merely superficial. He finds comfort in such clichés as "young people were always rebellious," or "the more things change, the more they stay the same."

An unknowing victim of future shock, the Denier sets himself up for personal catastrophe. His strategy for coping increases the likelihood that when he is finally forced to adapt, his encounter with change will come in the form of a single massive life crisis

rather than a sequence of manageable problems.

A second strategy of the future-shock victim is specialism. The Specialist doesn't block out *all* novel ideas or information, but attempts instead to keep pace with change in a specific narrow sector of life. Thus we witness the spectacle of the physician or financier who makes use of all the latest innovations in his profession, but remains rigidly closed to any suggestion for social, political, or economic innovation. The more universities undergo paroxysms of protest, the more ghettos go up in flames, the less the Specialist wants to know about them and the more closely he narrows the slit through which he sees the world. Superficially he copes well. But he, too, is running up the odds against himself. He may awake one morning to find that his specialty has become obsolete.

A third common response to future shock is obsessive reversion to formerly successful adaptations that are now irrelevant. The Reversionist sticks to his previously programmed decisions like a tramcar to its rails. The more urgently he is threatened by change from without, the more meticulously he repeats past modes of action. His social outlook is regressive. Shocked by the arrival of the future, he offers hysterical support for the not-so status quo, or he demands, in one masked form or another, a return to the glories of yesteryear.

The Barry Goldwaters and George Wallaces of the world appeal to his gut through the politics of nostalgia. He craves the slower pace of the agricultural past, the comprehensibility of small-town life. If parents would only quit sparing the rod, if the police would crush a few more skulls, if children were taught respect for God, Country, and Mother, all would once more return to the splendid normalcy of yesterday.

Not all Reversionists are so unsophisticated, nor are all of them to be found on the political right. The same glorification of the past infects the various hippie offshoots and the New Left as well. This accounts for youth's current fascination with rural communes and for the heavy component of pastoral imagery in their poetry, movies, and posters. The same bucolic romanticism tinges their attitude toward nontechnological nations and motivates their technophobia. For all their fiery demands for change, at least some members of the left share with the Wallacites and Goldwaterites a secret passion for the past.

Just as the youngsters' Indian headbands, their Edwardian capes, their Deerslayer boots, and their gold-rimmed glasses mimic various eras of the past, so, too, do their ideas. Turn-of-the-century terrorism and quaint Black Flag anarchy are suddenly back in vogue. The Rousseauean cult of the noble savage flourishes anew. Antique Marxist ideas, applicable at best to yesterday's industrialism, are hauled out as solutions for the problems of tomorrow's superindustrialism. Reversionism masquerades as revolution.

Finally, we have the Supersimplifier, who, with the world exploding around him, frantically seeks a single neat equation that will explain all the complex novelties. This helps account for the rampant intellectual faddism that already threatens to outpace the rate of turnover in fashion. McLuhan? Prophet of the electric age! Lévi-Strauss? Wow! Marcuse? Now I see it all! The Maharishi of Whatchamacallit? Fantastic! Astrology? Insight of the ages!

Groping desperately for an intellectual handhold in a society collapsing under his feet, the Supersimplifier invests every idea he comes across with universal relevance. Maximization of profits explains America. The Communist Conspiracy explains race riots. Participatory democracy is the answer to all ills. Permissiveness (or Dr. Spock) is the root of all evil.

This search for a unitary solution at the intellectual level has its parallels in action. Thus the bewildered, anxious student, pressured by parents, uncertain of his draft status, nagged at by an educational system whose obsolescence is more strikingly revealed every day, forced to decide on a career, a set of values, and a worthwhile life-style, searches wildly for a way to simplify his existence. By taking LSD, methedrine, or heroin he performs an illegal act that has, at least, the virtue of consolidating his miseries. He trades a host of seemingly insoluble troubles for one big problem, thus radically if temporarily simplifying existence.

Violence, too, offers a "simple" way out of general overstimulation and increasing complexity of choice. For the older generation and the political establishment, police truncheons and military bayonets loom as attractive remedies, a way to end dissent once and for all. Black extremists and white vigilantes both employ violence to narrow their choices and clarify their lives. For those who lack an intelligent, comprehensive program, who cannot cope with the novelties and complexities of blinding change, terrorism substitutes for thought. Terrorism may not topple regimes, but it removes doubts.

Most of us can quickly spot these patterns of behavior in others—even in ourselves—without at the same time understanding their causes. Yet information scientists will instantly recognize denial, specialization, reversion, and supersimplification as classical

techniques for coping with overload.

All these techniques dangerously evade the rich complexity of reality. They generate distorted images of reality. The more the individual denies, the more he specializes at the expense of wider interests, the more mechanically he reverts to past habits and policies, the more desperately he supersimplifies—the more inept his responses will be to the novelty and choices flooding into his life. The more he relies on these strategies, the more his behavior will exhibit wild and erratic swings and general instability.

Every information scientist recognizes that some of these strategies may indeed be necessary in overload situations. Yet, unless the individual begins with a clear grasp of relevant reality, and unless he begins with cleanly defined values and priorities, his reliance on such techniques will only deepen his adaptive difficulties.

These preconditions, however, are increasingly difficult to meet. Thus, the future-shock victim who does employ these strategies experiences a deepening sense of confusion and uncertainty. Caught in the turbulent flow of change, called upon to make significant, rapid-fire life decisions, he feels not simply intellectual bewilderment but disorientation at the level of personal values. As the pace of change quickens, this confusion is tinged with self-doubt, anxiety, and fear. He grows tense, tires easily; he may fall ill. As the pressures relentlessly mount, tension shades into irritability, anger, and sometimes, senseless violence. Little events trigger enormous responses; large events bring inadequate responses.

The confusion and uncertainty brought on by rising levels of transience, novelty, and diversity in our environment may explain the profound apathy that desocializes millions, old and young alike. This is not the studied, temporary withdrawal of the sensible person who needs to unwind or slow down before coping anew with his problems. It is total surrender before the strain of decision-making in conditions of uncertainty and overchoice.

For the first time in history affluence allows large numbers of people to make their withdrawal a full-time proposition. On the beach at Matala, a tiny sun-drenched village in Crete, there are forty or fifty caves occupied by runaway American troglodytes, young men and women who for the most part have given up any further effort to cope with the exploding complexities of life in the midst of high-speed change. Here decisions are few, and time plentiful. Here the choices are narrowed. No problem of overstimulation. No need to comprehend or even to feel. A reporter visiting them in 1968 brought news of the assassination of Robert F. Kennedy. Their response: silence. "No shock, no rage, no tears. Is this the new phenomenon? Running away from America and running away from emotion? I understand uninvolvement, disenchantment, even noncommitment. But where has all the feeling gone?"

The reporter might be able to understand where all the feeling has gone if he understood the impact of overstimulation: the apathy of the Chindit guerrilla, the blank face of the disaster victim, the withdrawal of the culture-shock victim. For these young people, and millions of others—the confused, the violent, and the apathetic—already evince the intellectual and emotional symptoms of future shock. They are its earliest victims.

It is impossible to produce future shock in large numbers of individuals without affecting the rationality of the society as a whole. Today, according to Daniel Patrick Moynihan, the chief White House advisor on urban affairs, the United States increasingly "exhibits the qualities of an individual going through a nervous breakdown." For the cumulative impact of sensory, cognitive, or decisional overstimulation, not to mention the physical effects of neural or endocrine overload, creates sickness in our midst.

This sickness is increasingly mirrored in our culture, our philosophy, our attitude toward reality. It is no accident that so many ordinary people refer to the world as a "madhouse" or that the theme of insanity has recently become a staple in literature, art, and drama. The assertion that the world has "gone crazy," the graffiti slogan "reality is a crutch," the interest in hallucinogenic drugs, the enthusiasm for astrology and occultism, the search for truth in sensation, ecstasy, and "peak experience," the swing toward extreme subjectivism, the attacks on science, the snowballing belief that reason has failed man, all reflect the everyday experience of ordinary people who find they can no longer cope rationally with change.

Millions sense the pathology that pervades the air, but fail to understand its roots. These roots lie not in this or that political doctrine, still less in some mystical core of despair or isolation presumed to inhere in the "human condition." Nor do they lie in science, technology, or legitimate demands for social change. They are traceable, instead, to the uncontrolled, nonselective nature of our lunge into the future. They lie in our failure to direct consciously and imaginatively the advance toward superindustrialism.

Thus, despite its extraordinary achievements in art, in science, and in intellectual, moral, and political life, the United States is a nation in which

tens of thousands of young people flee reality by opting for drug-induced lethargy; a nation in which millions of their parents retreat into a video-induced stupor or an alcoholic haze; a nation in which legions of elderly folk vegetate and die in loneliness; in which the flight from family and occupational responsibility has become an exodus; in which masses tame their raging anxieties with Miltown, or Librium, or Equanil, or a score of other tranquilizers and psychic pacifiers. Such a nation, whether it knows it or not, is suffering from future shock.

Lest Europeans or Japanese or Russians rest smugly on their presumed sanity, however, it is well to ask whether similar symptoms are not already present in their societies, too. Are Americans unique in this respect, or are they simply suffering the initial brunt of an assault on the psyche that will soon stagger other nations as well?

Rooted in human biology and physiology, and in the rate and character of change, future shock reminds us that our brains and bodies, in their present forms, can tolerate only so much stress. When forced beyond the limits of our tolerance, we respond with the erratic behavior that is the hallmark of future shock.

Social rationality presupposes individual rationality, and this, in turn, depends not only on certain biological equipment but on continuity, order, and regularity in the environment. It is premised on some correlation between the pace and complexity of change and man's decisional capacities. By blindly stepping up the rate of change, the level of novelty, and the extent of of choice, we are condemning millions to future shock. We are thoughtlessly tampering with the environmental preconditions of rationality.

A "social futurist," Alvin Toffler is a visiting scholar at the Russell Sage Foundation. The foregoing essay is adapted from his book Future Shock, *to be published this spring by Random House, Inc.*

GREAT CONFRONTATIONS:
Leo X and Luther

"God has given us the Papacy, now let us enjoy it." The words may never have been spoken, but they are unforgettable. History will forever remember Leo X as the pope who presided in cultured splendor over the dissolution of the medieval Catholic Church. Time has not been kind to Giovanni de' Medici, whose family purchased him a cardinal's hat at fourteen and who was elected pope in 1513 at the age of thirty-seven. His own generation, however, applauded the elevation of a restful and generous man of exquisite taste and powerful connections who would "act as a gentle lamb rather than as a fierce lion" and would promote peace, not war.

The civilized world may have thought him a trifle young to fill Saint Peter's chair —cardinals preferred to elevate their septuagenarian colleagues on the sound principle that the higher the turnover, the greater their own chances of election. But Leo X did not disappoint his supporters, who judged the new pontiff in terms of his immediate predecessors: Innocent VIII (1484–1492), who had blatantly purchased his tiara and whose family spent his pontificate seeking a reasonable return on their investment; Alexander VI (1492–1503), who with the help of his son and daughter, Cesare and Lucrezia Borgia, turned God's high vicarage into a carnival of political and personal immorality; and Julius II (1503–1513), the tough, old warrior pope who in-

In Raphael's portrait a myopic Leo X holds the magnifying glass he always kept at hand. His nephew, the future Clement VII, is at left.

timidated most of Europe with his martial zeal. In contrast, Giovanni de' Medici earned his election without benefit of golden florin, was "careful of his honor and good repute," and sought to become the mediator, not the scourge, of Europe. Yet Leo, not Innocent, Alexander, or Julius, is remembered as the pope who fiddled while Christendom went up in flames. The avarice, perversion, and heavy-fisted aggression of his predecessors are scarcely recalled at all, but the frivolousness of a highly intelligent man who refused to take Martin Luther

seriously has never been forgiven or forgotten.

There was, of course, an element of bad luck—Martin Luther happened to post his Ninety-Five Theses during Leo's administration—but even so, the pope probably deserves his reputation. More than any other Renaissance pontiff he epitomized the spiritual sterility that was spreading through the old church. Pope, cardinal, bishop, priest, all were emotionally emasculated technicians; they could not sense the intensity of despair, love, faith, and hate that made it impossible for some men to countenance life with its multitude of petty abuses and sordid secular ways. They were what William James called "healthy-minded" men in matters of religion, men who never found cause to ask: what am I doing in an eternity of space and time? Personally Leo was not an irreligious man. He worshiped his God with confidence and respect; as the Venetian ambassador said, "he fulfills his religious duties conscientiously, but he will live and enjoy life," as only a Renaissance prince could afford. His was the generation of the intellectual intoxication of the Eternal City, which only sixty years before had been called a community of cowherds and now was a temple of art and erudition.

There is something deeply disturbing about the character of this Renaissance pope. The mind can handle the cruelty

By LACEY BALDWIN SMITH

"It is one of the most tragic ironies of history" that Leo X, a spiritual eunuch, "should have been called upon to handle one of the lustiest Christians of all times: Martin Luther"

of Alexander, the greed of Innocent, and the fury of Julius, but not the ambivalence of Leo. He arranged gastronomic orgies for his guests and stuffed them with peacocks' tongues, apes' meat, and ravens' flesh, but he himself ate sparingly, only one meal a day, and fasted three days a week. He was spectacularly generous to art and to scholarship as well as to the poor, hated to say no, and always sought to soften a blow with a kind word, but he condoned the cruelest kind of buffoonery and permitted the ridicule of poets who had been deliberately led to believe themselves geniuses. He was a man who was chaste in his private life, but who financed an elaborate and public verseplay during the spring carnival of 1521 in which a woman prayed to Venus to send her a lover and was obliged with eight hermits who conveniently turned into robust young men and fought one another to the death for her charms, the sole survivor receiving the prize. Finally, he was a pope who startled his ecclesiastical colleagues after his election by actually washing and kissing the feet of the poor on Maundy Thursday, but who is said to have dismissed one of the stories of Christ's life as "a profitable fable." Over and over again contemporaries reported that the pontiff sought to remove everything unpleasant from sight and mind, to gild reality with a veneer of art, learning, and diplomacy, and

A rugged miner's son, Martin Luther was painted by Lucas Cranach in 1526 wearing the subdued garments of a university professor.

NATIONALMUSEUM, STOCKHOLM

to live life, as it were, vicariously. As the eunuch who directs the affairs of the harem is sexually impotent, so Leo, who presided over an institution that spoke for the heart and soul of Christendom, was emotionally dead to the desire that stands at the core of a Christian's response to God. It is one of the most tragic ironies of history that such a pope should have been called upon to handle one of the lustiest Christians of all times: Martin Luther.

Though the eunuch repels, he may be an excellent human being, and Leo was neither an evil man nor a bad pope. For all the "jests and amusements" in which he delighted, he never forgot the duties of his office; but they were the visible and political burdens of a head of state, not the inward and spiritual responsibilities of God's vicar on earth. His aims were admirable, and in the first year of his reign he made his purposes clear: to bring peace to Christendom, prevent fresh wars in Italy, preserve the independence of the Papal States, and unite the Great Powers in defense of Europe against the infidel. The political world of Leo X included the Most Christian King of France, His Most Catholic Majesty of Spain, the Defender of the Faith, Harry of England, and the weightiest dignity of them all, the Holy Roman Emperor. Leo was the spiritual father of this dangerous band of well-bred but hungry sovereign-cannibals who were always careful to say grace before consuming one of their less powerful fellows.

Of the kingdoms of Europe, France with her sixteen million hard-working peasants and artisans was the most powerful, and Spain, newly constructed out of the dynastic union of Aragon and Castile and forged in the age-old conflict with Islam, was the most dynamic; but the Holy Roman Empire, rickety and shattered as it was, remained in theory, if not in fact, the paramount power of Christendom.

For centuries pope and emperor had struggled to dominate the medieval world; each claimed to be the rightful heir of Rome, each sought universal supremacy, the one spiritual, the other political, and in the end each was forced to retreat before the growing power of the territorial princes of Europe. By the sixteenth century the Holy Roman Empire was wholly German, Roman only in the minds of the popes, and imperial solely in name. The empire was hopelessly splintered into more than six hundred political fragments, and the imperial office was elective—the creature of the four secular Electors of Bohemia, Brandenburg, the Palatinate, and Saxony and the three spiritual Electors of Cologne, Mainz, and Treves. Yet the past dies hard; the imperial crown continued to "outshine all other worldly titles," the legend of universal monarchy persisted, and Leo can scarcely be blamed for allowing a political myth to enter into his diplomatic reckonings. With revenues more extensive than those of Henry Tudor and a potential for war greater than any other Italian state, no one, least of all Leo, seriously doubted that the papacy was a vital part of the historic international establishment and had territorial and economic interests to protect as weighty as those of any other sovereign state.

Leo was the perfect statesman-pope. Urbane, gracious, flexible, and forever avoiding irrevocable decisions on the time-honored premise that international issues are never solved but are merely replaced by more pressing problems, he adroitly negotiated the diplomatic course, always, it was said, "steering by two compasses." With a hint of a smile for one to show his double meaning, a polite Latin verse for another to give him time for thought, or a ring from his soft, snow-white fingers to win an important friend, he sought to maintain the European balance of power and protect the political interests of the papacy in Italy. There were, of course, other considerations: his precious city of Flor-

ence had to be defended against French schemes to restore the republic and evict his nephew, young Lorenzo de' Medici; the family welfare of his three sisters and endless Medici cousins had to be assured; and most time-consuming and delicate of all, the papacy's position in France had to be worked out to the satisfaction of both pope and king.

Leo conceived of the church as a vast, vulnerable, and universal organization with revenues, real estate, offices, and prestige in every kingdom of Europe that could be protected only if the realities of power were recognized. Maneuvering within this framework, he negotiated with France a bargain that faced the facts of political life. For decades the French kings had controlled the chief ecclesiastical appointments and the revenues of the Gallic church; now, by the Concordat of Bologna in 1516, the pope recognized the Crown's rights and in return won for the papacy and the theory of papal supremacy its firmest ally. Far more adroitly than any dangerous clerical reform that might have antagonized the great and the powerful, the Concordat kept France both Catholic and papal. Shrewd politics, not reform, was Leo's panacea for a church that lived in a world of predatory monarchs, national ecclesiastical structures that lost little love on the Curia, and territorial prelates who thought of themselves as, and in fact frequently were, independent princes.

Under the circumstances there was little time in Leo's busy day for theological scholars, university students, and humanistic propagandists nagging about ecclesiastical abuses, those trifling social and moral aberrations that invariably attach themselves to any venerable and comfortable institution. Germany had been fulminating against Rome for decades, and a pope could not be expected to listen to everyone who disliked paying taxes. The papal head might appear to some to be too lofty, but the world's largest business

could not be run without cost—both spiritual and financial—and anyone like the German humanist Ulrich von Hutten, who described Rome as "the great barn of the universe, into which is garnered all that has been robbed and taken from other nations" and the pope as "that insatiable corn-weevil which devours piles of fruit, surrounded by its many fellow-gluttons," did his cause little good by such gross exaggerations. Moreover, as that fateful day in October of 1517 approached, when a university professor would nail his defiance to a Wittenberg church door, there was a far more pressing and pleasurable matter to settle, the construction of that supreme monument to God in heaven and to Renaissance engineering and good taste on earth: St. Peter's Cathedral, the architectural embodiment of Leo's image of the church militant—intricate, balanced, and majestic.

St. Peter's, parts of which were a thousand years old, was in imminent danger of collapsing, and Julius II had already begun its demolition in preparation for a total rebuilding. A year after his accession Leo called on Raphael to submit new designs and act as chief architect. With his usual immodesty, the painter made no effort to depreciate his plans: "This is certainly the first church in the world, and the greatest building that man has ever yet seen; the cost will amount to a million in gold." Money, of course, was the rub. Julius had issued a special St. Peter's indulgence to raise funds, and now Leo extended its operation to include Portugal, most of France, and large sections of Germany, but he exempted the possessions of Albert, the archbishop of Mainz and Magdeburg, under whose ecclesiastical jurisdiction the city of Wittenberg and the northern areas of the electorate of Saxony fell. In March of 1515, however, Leo negotiated with Albert a mutually agreeable understanding that has stood ever since as a baleful monument to everything that was wrong with the sixteenth-century ecclesia.

It is extremely easy to get lost in the technical aspects of indulgences. Suffice it to say that they were remissions granted by the church of the temporal penalties of sin. They applied both to penance on earth and to punishment in purgatory, were granted in return for some good work (monetary or otherwise), and were originally issued for the benefit of those who went crusading on Christ's behalf and fell in battle. Over the course of centuries the practice, if not the theory, became dangerously commercialized, until indulgences were regarded as a form of spiritual investment by the purchaser and a useful source of revenue by the church.

Both Leo and Albert were extremely interested in exactly how many florins the faithful could be persuaded to give, and a graduated order of expectations was drawn up ranging from twenty-five gold florins for royalty to half a florin for the poor. The pope sought to immortalize the church in stone, and half the returns were allotted to the magnificent edifice of St. Peter's, but Albert had more secular requirements to finance. He wanted to compensate himself and his family for the immense cost of holding three dioceses at once. The archbishop was the brother of one of the seven Electors of the empire, Joachim I, Elector of Brandenburg, and he had been installed as Archbishop of Magdeburg at the uncanonical age of twenty-two. A year later, in 1514, he was elected through family influence to the far more important archbishopric of Mainz, the senior ecclesiastical electorate of the empire, and he asked Leo for permission to hold both archdioceses along with the see of Halberstadt. The pope was not opposed to princely prelates in theory, but he hesitated to sanction such a glaring example of pluralism. Ultimately, however, politics swayed His Holiness. The Holy Roman Emperor could not live forever, and the election of his successor was of great political interest to Leo; the loyalty of two of the imperial Electors was certainly worth a slight stretching of canon law.

So the bargain was arranged—fourteen thousand ducats (some authorities say twenty-one thousand) for the regular entrance fees and another ten thousand as compensation for a special dispensation to hold three dioceses at once. To help Albert, whose new diocese of Mainz was nearly bankrupt, borrow this huge sum from the banking house of Jacob Fugger, the Curia permitted him to sell indulgences in his territories for eight years, half the income to go to Rome to rebuild St. Peter's, and half to Albert to repay the Fuggers. Almost no one in Rome seriously questioned the means or the ends of this amicable arrangement, which was on a par with those quiet agreements whereby modern princes of industry and finance seek to avoid taxation by turning over securities to universities while retaining the use of the income. Such are the ways of the world, and such are the means by which cathedrals, libraries, and laboratories are built.

It took months to work out the details of this delicate scheme, and it was not until early 1517 that the famous Dominican monk John Tetzel was ready to preach the indulgence, but in the meantime Frederick, Elector of Saxony, had prohibited any selling of indulgences in his lands. His motives add yet another dimension to the story, for they were inspired more by professional jealousy than by reforming zeal. At Wittenberg the Elector had gathered together one of the most spectacular collections of relics to be found in Europe—four hairs from the Virgin's head, fourteen scraps of her clothing, a wisp of straw from the manger, a strand of Christ's beard, a nail from the Cross, and some 19,013 sacred bones, the whole of which, if venerated in the proper spirit and accompanied by a small monetary token, could cut 1,902,202 years and 270 days from the pains of purgatory. Possibly it is not unjust to say that when Tetzel approached within a mile of Wittenberg,

Europe was confronted with the clash of two rival and extremely profitable "spiritual crusades." What happened next is common knowledge; a rather insignificant university professor of theology with a sense of spiritual outrage matched only by the magnificence of his propaganda posted his Ninety-Five Theses on October 31, 1517, the eve of All Saint's Day, the city's principal holiday, when great crowds of pilgrims piled into the church to view the relics. With a single bang of the hammer Luther toppled forever the careful political schemes and considerations of Leo X.

Luther was no child of the Renaissance. He had visited Rome only three years before Leo became pope and had found the Eternal City disgusting. While Giovanni de' Medici was being exposed to a classical-humanistic education befitting the second son of Lorenzo the Magnificent, Martin Luther, eight years his junior, was just becoming aware of who he was—the second son of a tough, hard-sweating, unpretentious mine owner only one generation removed from the soil, who by dint of simple living and long hours had managed to haul himself and his eight children up into the ranks of the petty bourgeoisie. When Giovanni's world was falling in about him and Florence in 1494 evicted the Medicis bag and baggage, Big Hans Luther was still scraping together the silver to fulfill his ambitions for his brilliant son— grammar school at Magdeburg, then on to the university at Erfurt, and finally law school, a splendid marriage, a comfortable legal practice, and a family of fat babies. Martin, in fact, almost completed his father's social dream, but in 1505, a short time after entering law school, he quit the society of man and joined the Augustinian friars. Thus, while the exiled Medici was making his way at Rome, acquiring the art of political survival at the courts of Alexander VI and Julius II, the exiled Luther was learning how to talk to his Deity. Neither man found the going easy, but Giovanni de' Medici rolled with the punches, believed in his stars, and by 1513 had become a skilled politician and liberal patron of the arts. In contrast, the German monk fought the whole way, and monastic life almost destroyed him in his struggle to make peace with his God. As Leo was taking up his pontifical burdens and pleasures, Luther was appointed permanently to the faculty of Wittenberg and began to move slowly out of the darkness of despair into the light of new hope. Man, he discovered, is saved by his faith alone; he need not struggle to be worthy of God's forgiveness, for he can never deserve salvation; he cannot earn paradise or make a deal to attain it; instead, God, through Christ's atonement, extends his mercies to all men irrespective of merit.

If Leo was the "healthy-minded" man, Luther was the perfect image of William James's "sick soul," calling out for aid in his terror and finding it in a direct and intensely personal relationship between God and man that had nothing to do with indulgences, good works, priests, tithes, churches built of stone, or the entire edifice of the church militant. The formula—justification by faith alone—was innocent enough, but in the hands of a generation already dismayed by a church in which it was impossible to isolate the corruption, the phrase became the prescription for sweeping away all the frustrations of the past and calling in the golden age of the Apostles.

Historical comparisons are dangerous, but in the collision between Leo and Luther a modern parallel jumps to mind. One is reminded of the explosive encounter between the university president, who is skilled at handling his trustees, spends his days raising money for libraries, faculty salaries, and student scholarships, and is responsible for running an incredibly complex organization whose very existence depends on a tactful balancing of the principle of freedom of thought with the needs and wishes of society as a whole, and the activist or nihilistic student, who dismisses laboratories, dormitories, athletics, and the existing curriculum as flimsy window-dressing for a thoroughly obsolete social system and demands the total rejuvenation of all aspects of life. The language of protest and the circumstances in the twentieth century are very different from those of the sixteenth, but the gulf that divides the idealist, be he a theological professor or a sociology major, from the realist, be he pope or university president, remains the same: they simply define reality from totally different perspectives. In the case of Leo and Luther each man sought the welfare of the church according to his own principles, and together they succeeded in bringing a thousand-year-old institution crashing down.

The revolutionary implications of Luther's Ninety-Five Theses were self-evident, and Number 81 struck at the heart of the matter: "This unbridled preaching of indulgences makes it difficult for learned men to guard the respect due to the Pope against false accusations, or at least from the keen criticisms of the laity." Respect stood at the core of ecclesiastical discipline and obedience, and once respect was destroyed, the whole impressive structure, of which the pope was the apex, collapsed. If, as Luther was suggesting, indulgences were unnecessary, then what about the usefulness of all good works; if good works were questioned, then what about the doctrine of man's free will and his ability to choose or reject God; if the pope could not call upon the church's reservoir of grace to remit the penalities of sin in purgatory, then what were the pope's powers, if any? Did purgatory really exist; and what was the treasury of the ecclesia beyond the Word of God as recorded in Scripture? So the questions and doubts spread steadily outward, first to challenge obedience to Rome and finally to engulf the entire codex of Catholic theology.

Very possibly nothing could have stopped the spread: the rot in the old church had gone too far, hatred of Rome in the minds of the laity was too intense, the financial and political interests of the German princes were too strong, the spiritual anguish of Christians had been ignored too long, and the generation gap was too great (Luther's most devout converts were the young students and monks of the universities and monasteries). But Leo's handling of the crisis certainly did not help.

Albert of Mainz promptly sent Luther's theses to Rome "with the good hope that His Holiness would grasp the situation so as to meet the error at once." Leo did almost nothing. He could not perceive anything more significant than an Augustinian Luther and a Dominican Tetzel engaging in a noisy and unedifying monastic squabble and an Elector endeavoring to safeguard his own reliquary revenues by depreciating the indulgences of the pope. Moreover, a vast international crisis was brewing, for the old emperor Maximilian was close to death, and his heir was a matter of supreme importance to the pope. Leo felt that he had to prevent at any cost the election of Charles, monarch of the combined kingdoms of Aragon and Castile, king of Naples, and duke of Burgundy, as Maximilian's successor, for it would bring the Holy Roman Empire into Italy, and the border of Naples was only forty miles from the city of Rome itself. Worse, the delicate balance that Leo had been striving to maintain between Spain, France, England, and the Empire would be smashed if a single sovereign succeeded in uniting the imperial crown with the commerical wealth of the Burgundian lowlands and the disciplined peasant-infantry of Spain. It was crucial to the welfare of the papacy that Charles be stopped and that some other candidate be found, and the man whom Leo preferred above all others was Martin Luther's overlord, that wily old politician, the Elector of Saxony, a point that bedeviled the pontiff's handling of Luther's heresy almost from the start.

Events now began to move too fast

and too violently even for Leo's skillful manipulation. On February 3, 1518, the pope ordered the vicar general of the Augustinian Order to discipline his erstwhile brother and muzzle his heresies, but in April of 1518, when Luther traveled to Heidelberg for the triennial convention of his order, he found a friendly welcome among Augustinians who held the Dominicans in contempt. The Dominicans answered in June by instituting formal canonical proceedings against Luther at Rome. At best a papal investigation moved slowly, and not until early August did Luther receive his summons to the Holy City, whereupon the Wittenberg professor appealed to Frederick to defend the honor of his university. The Elector, despite his museum of sacred bones, had no intention of delivering his distinguished, if dangerous, professor to the doubtful mercies of the Roman Curia and bluntly ignored the pope's request that Luther be arrested and sent to the Vatican for a trial. Instead he demanded that Martin have an impartial hearing in Germany. Leo was in no position to argue with an imperial Elector, and in October, his expenses paid by Frederick, the Wittenberg theologian set forth to do battle before the pope's legate at the Imperial Diet of Augsburg. The result was scarcely propitious; instead of bringing the heretic to obedience, the encounter simply widened the gulf, for the legate ended by appealing to the historic authority of the church, and Luther to his own interpretation of Scripture. The debate was civilized and polite, but Luther was advised to flee secretly back to Wittenberg and the protection of the Elector, who continued to argue that no one as yet had proved his professor a heretic.

Luther's heresy was growing, but alas, so was the political crisis. While the disobedient monk was at Heidelberg in April, Leo got wind of Maximilian's plan to secure the election of his grandson Charles as his successor. Then, in January of 1519, the emperor died, and for the next six months the

theological opinions of Martin Luther were the very least of the pope's worries, for both Francis I of France and Charles of Spain were spending vast sums of money to purchase the support of the seven Electors of the empire, and Leo was appalled at the prospect of either becoming emperor. He preferred Francis to Charles, but in early June, when it became apparent that the German princes would never elect a French emperor, he began to push the name of Frederick, Elector of Saxony. To his credit the Elector was not interested, and on June 28, 1519, the inevitable happened: Charles was unanimously elected emperor.

More than a year and a half had slipped by since Luther nailed his theses to the church door, but even so, it was not until January 9, 1520, that proceedings against him were instituted. The mills of the Medici Curia ground exceeding slow but exceeding fine. Every avenue of compromise was investigated, both spiritual and political, and it was not until June 15 that the bull *Exsurge Domine* condemning Martin Luther's doctrines was ready for publication. In contrast to this single and rather anxious statement to the faithful, which began, "Let the Lord arise and his enemies be scattered," Luther's literary outpourings were a trumpet call to arms against Rome and the entire Catholic Church. By the end of the year he had produced twenty-four publications, had formulated all the basic tenets of his faith, and had delivered them with unparalleled force to the German people.

By June of 1520 it was far too late to stop Luther, let alone Lutheranism. Leo survived the debacle of his policies by scarcely a year; he died suddenly and mysteriously (possibly of malaria) at midnight on December 1, 1521, aged forty-six. By then Luther and half of Germany were in open revolt, and the Wittenberg professor had caught the imagination of history when at the Diet of Worms on April 18, 1521, he had informed the young em-

peror: "I cannot and I will not recant anything, for to go against conscience is neither right nor safe. God help me. Amen. Here I stand, I cannot do otherwise." His words have probably been improved upon with the telling, but his message was clear and memorable. As for Leo X, he is almost forgotten except for the single searing point that because it happened during his administration, he was responsible; and so he was—symbolically.

History was to prove Luther triumphant. Perhaps the worm at the core of the old church had indeed gone too deep for the edifice to be repaired without major demolition and rebuilding. Leo's only remedy had been to apply fresh paint and to cover up the cracks, but in retrospect it may be well to remember that he saw the church in terms of its political façade and that exteriors require paint far more often than interiors need new rafters and floorboards. Few people, of course, realized at the time that the old building was falling down upon them, but when Giovanni de' Medici died, men did sense that a way of life, an approach to living, was in the process of disappearing. Shortly there would be no room for the urbane, cultured, and ephemeral men of Leo's world, as a new generation of ruthless idealists took over, reformers in both camps whose faith plunged Europe into a hundred years of religious war. Possibly Giovio Paolo had cause to write: "now that this great prince has departed, we perforce must mourn under an age of iron inasmuch as, through our mistakes and failures, barbarous savagery has brought upon us murder, pestilence, hunger, desolation—in short, all human evils; knowledge, art, the common well-being, the joy of living—in a word, all good things have gone down into the grave along with Leo."

Lacey Baldwin Smith, a professor of history at Northwestern University, wrote on the Wars of the Roses in the Winter, 1969, issue of HORIZON. *He is presently at work on a biography of Henry VIII.*

This Danish farming village of around 200 B.C. has been carefully reconstructed on the basis of archaeological evidence alone; just as carefully one of the houses was set afire (below) to find out if it would make a plausible ruin.

AN EXPERIMENT WITH TIME

At a new Danish research center, archaeologists—and multitudes of others—are learning how life really was lived two thousand years ago

Twenty-five miles west of Copenhagen and only five miles beyond Roskilde, where the kings of Denmark have been buried since 1400, lies a village whose connections with the kings of Denmark go back, according to legend, three times as far as Roskilde. The village of Lejre (pronounced lie-ray) now basks in rural peace, but if we are to believe the tenth-century sagas and the eighth-century Anglo-Saxon epic *Beowulf*, Lejre had been for some centuries the fortress residence of the legendary kings of Denmark and had around A.D. 500 witnessed many a scene of battle and sudden death. Here the sons of King Skjold had waged their internecine feuds, here Rolf Krake and his twelve berserkers had fought and outwitted the king of Sweden and years later had died fighting in the blazing ruins of their stockaded hall.

Nothing is left aboveground to show where Rolf's fortress stood, but all around Lejre lie the relics of a later age, the Viking period of the last pre-Christian kings. The large flat-topped tumuli and the ship-shaped crescents of standing stones that mark the burial places of Viking chieftains crowd thick about Lejre.

If you drive through the village, you may spot an unobtrusive signboard bearing a stylized ash-tree—the Ygdrasil of Norse mythology—and the inscription "To the Archaeological Research Center." Signs will lead you for three miles across rolling wooded country to the site of a project begun in 1964 by a student of archaeology, Hans-Ole Hansen, with backing from the Carlsberg Foundation, that remarkable institution that runs a brewery solely to finance research in the arts, the humanities, and the purer forms of science. The purpose of the research center is unique. For decades archaeologists have tried to bring to their work—the study of prehistory—the spirit and methods of science. But the guiding principle of natural science, that theory should be checked by experiment, has in the nature of things been difficult to incorporate into the techniques of archaeology. The Lejre center was started to try to do just that.

The experiments conducted at Lejre are of two kinds. The first consists in testing the interpretations of what is dug up from the earth. Can a flint "scraper" really scrape skins? Can the clay structures normally interpreted as meat-smoking ovens really smoke meat, or the so-called pottery kilns fire pottery? By erecting posts in the pattern of the post-holes of an Iron Age house, do you get a real structure? And

Archaeologist Hans-Ole Hansen, wielding a tape recorder instead of a spade, tapes his observations of one of the house-burnings.

By GEOFFREY BIBBY

97

if so, can you live in it? Is the pattern of potsherds in the ruins of a burned-out prehistoric house consistent with the pots having been standing on a shelf? And if so, how high was the shelf from the ground? What type of plow, used in what way, would produce the furrow marks found on the subsoil below Stone Age tumuli?

The second class of experiments involves the determination of prehistoric ways of life from archaeological facts. Given the known type of corn grown in the Neolithic period, and the known implements of tillage, harvesting, and milling of the period, what would be the yield in grain per acre of ground? Or alternatively, what acreage would be necessary to support a family of, say, six? Given the looms attested by archaeology, how many man-hours would be needed to produce, for example, the Huldremose robe, one of the finest of the Iron Age garments found in the Danish peat bogs?

Work is concentrated on the Iron Age, which is archaeologically the best documented period of Danish prehistory. It is the period from about 500 B.C. to about A.D. 300, when first Celts and then Romans dominated Europe south of Denmark, the period during which two Danish tribes, the Cimbri and the Teutones, made a brief and warlike incursion into southern Europe and the pages of history.* Weapon hoards and weapon burials within Denmark itself testify to the frequency of intertribal wars and interfamily feuds, but life, though never free from the threat of violence, was not one of constant warfare. The Roman historian Tacitus, in his *Germania,* has given us a picture of the peasant life of northern Europe, of the hardy beer-drinking but somewhat puritanical communities where each village was ruled by its council of elders and where the gods of the forests, the lakes, and the peat mosses were very much present. The evidence of archaeology bears out this picture. There are the fields, carved out of heath and woodland by the

*See "The Celts," HORIZON, Spring, 1965.

new iron-coltered plow, the occasional earth-ramparted fort, and the innumerable villages, with their cobbled streets winding among the sites of a dozen or so houses. And in the peat bogs are the offerings to the gods: black pottery vessels; the long, fair tresses of the women and the swords and shields of the men; the slaughtered animals and the slaughtered men.*

Archaeology, however, has its limits. We do not actually know what Iron Age houses looked like. All we have to go on are their ground-level remains. So we know a lot about their ground plans and their floors; we know that the houses were long and narrow, with clay floors and a hearth in the western end, where the family lived, and with cattle stables, sometimes cobbled, in the eastern half. We know something of the walling, of wattle and daub, often reinforced with walls of turf, and we can locate the double row of posts down the center of the house that must have supported the roof. But the actual roof construction is nowhere revealed. Here at once was scope for experiment.

A working party of eighty young volunteers of many nations erected in the course of the summer of 1964 six "Iron Age" houses. They followed the ground plans of known Iron Age houses, putting in adze-hewn timbers where they found post-holes. And they added roofs of varying pitches, thatched with reeds or with heather or covered with turf.

As soon as the houses were built, certain old preconceptions began to be shaken. The hole in the roof always thought to exist above the hearth proved impossible to construct in such a way that smoke could escape without rain coming in, whereas a hole in the gable end of the house, beneath the peak of the roof, functioned perfectly. But the testing time came in the winter. Three hardy souls spent a fortnight living in the stoutest of the houses, together with a full complement of livestock, and proved that the houses as built were unfit for human habitation. It was not a subjective decision; it was

*See "The Body in the Bog," HORIZON, Winter, 1968.

For two wintry weeks a small "family" of volunteers lived in an "Iron Age" house and discovered it was too poorly constructed to keep them from freezing. Here, one of them prepares a meal in a kettle over the hearth.

based decisively on readings taken every three hours day and night from thermometers placed at varying heights in various parts of the house and compared with readings of temperature and wind strength and direction taken outside the house. Except for the area immediately around the hearth, sub-zero temperatures only slightly higher than the outside temperatures were recorded in far too many places. The fault proved to be uneven roof thatching, and by the second winter it was possible to build a habitable house.

Apart from this winter sojourn not much attempt was made to *live* in the houses. The experimental center was aiming at scientific objectivity in its experiments. The experimenters lived in the house not to find out what it felt like, for feelings cannot be measured, but because the thermometer readings would only give an accurate picture if the house was "manned" by a full complement of humans and domestic animals. Certain experiments were made in smoking meat and fish under the eaves. The stalls for the cattle, as deduced from excavations by archaeologists who were rarely stockmen, proved unsuitable, and a new construction had to be devised consistent with both the archaeological evidence and the habits of farmyard stock.

But mainly the "Iron Age" houses were built to be destroyed. During the five years of the center's existence some of the original houses have been maintained and two new ones have been built to test new theories. One has been left to itself and now stands abandoned, with its roof fallen in and its walls crumbling, reverting slowly to the condition in which, after all, archaeologists find Iron Age houses. Two have been burned to the ground—in both cases experimental replicas of houses that in reality burned down two thousand years ago. But this time the burning was scientifically controlled. Every piece of timber had metal numbers attached at intervals along its length; the exact positions of pottery and bags and

boxes of provisions were marked; the body of a dead calf was laid in the stalls. Then a match was applied. Twenty minutes later the roof collapsed as flames shot through the evening sky, and in little more than half an hour the house was a sunken heap of glowing timber. Its ruins lay undisturbed for a full year and then were excavated—by a professor of archaeology and a party of archaeological students who did *not* have access to the original plans of the house. The students were invited to "reconstruct" the house—this time on paper only—on the basis of the archaeological evidence.

In the meantime other experiments were taken up. Agriculture and stock-keeping became intimately connected. Experimental patches were sown with the various types of primitive grain—millet, emmer, einkorn, hulled and naked barley, and with other plants, such as flax, which were known to have grown at various periods of prehistory. But the plots had first to be plowed with replicas of the "ards," the colter-less plows found in the peat bogs of Denmark and Poland, and the plows had to be pulled by oxen and horses of types and sizes that resembled as closely as possible the breed current at the appropriate dates. The zoologists were able to give accurate skeletal measurements for prehistoric Danish domestic animals, and the hunt was on for their nearest living counterparts. Sheep from the Faroe Islands, cattle from northern Norway and Sweden, and horses from Norway and Iceland were collected, and the first breeding experiments were carried out, involving crossing the domestic pig and the wild boar to give an animal similar to the attested form of prehistoric pig. This opened up wider perspectives, and in unguarded moments the staff of the center talk of attempting to breed back to the aurochs, the great wild bull of the European forests that has long been extinct but whose blood is believed by many zoologists to run in certain breeds of domestic cattle.

The iron caldron and the girl are modern, but the dyes in which she dips her textiles are authentic for the Danish Iron Age and are made from herbs or leaves or tree bark that the students grow, or gather, themselves.

Students at the center are not encouraged to appear in costume, but this young man is trying out the products of the textile shop to see if they are warm, practical, and sturdy enough to have clothed an ancient Dane.

From time-and-motion studies of plowing with ards and oxen, it soon became obvious that the ard was no primitive implement; it could in skilled hands be adjusted to turn a very fine furrow—which had been believed to be impossible without a colter. And the yield of the various plots could be measured not merely in terms of bushels per acre but also in terms of man-hours per bushel.

Experiments in pottery making were conducted to discover the composition of clay and the firing techniques and temperatures required to produce the characteristic vessels of the Stone Age, the Bronze Age, and the Iron Age. After two years of work in this field the products of the pottery laboratory became indistinguishable from the real thing; archaeologists voiced their concern at the production of "forgeries" so good that they would not be able to recognize them as such if they came across them during excavation. So from then on all clay used in the Lejre experiments was mixed with tiny quantities of a rare earth found only in Greenland, which shows clearly fluorescent under ultraviolet light.

Weaving and dyeing were also closely related fields for experiment. Many specimens of textiles, including whole outfits of clothing from the Bronze and Iron ages, have been found in the Danish peat bogs and in hermetically sealed oak coffins. World-wide ethnological research had already gone into primitive loom-types. The Lejre center decided to find out whether certain looms could in fact produce fabrics identical with the prehistoric originals and at the same time how many hours of work were needed. And now the various spheres of research began to react upon each other: the "prehistoric" sheep of the livestock program furnished coarse wool of the required type, and one of the experimental plots of the agricultural program was planted with woad, the herb that produced the blue dye of the Iron Age. Other dyestuffs could be obtained from the woods at the research center

—oak leaves for brown, and willow and birch for green.

Several years were spent in learning to spin thread of the exact thickness, quality, and breaking strain of the Iron Age and in building and adjusting the looms to give the length of warp and weft and the number of threads to the inch that were found in the peat-bog garments. The greatest difficulty, perhaps, was encountered in building the round loom needed for the seamless robe from Huldremose, which was the first large-scale reproduction undertaken. But weavers could always find relaxation by experimenting with braiding and lacemaking techniques in their attempts to reproduce the hair ribbons and openwork caps of the ladies of the Bronze Age.

All these programs of scientific research were, of course, seriously conceived, carefully and meticulously planned and debated and carried through, with the primary aim of obtaining objective, demonstrable, measurable results. But it also turned out that they were fun, both for the participants and for the observers. For the experimenters, "subjectivity" was a constant and insidious trap—the belief that "living back," the feelings engendered by carrying out prehistoric activities with prehistoric implements in prehistoric surroundings, somehow had objective validity and could be treated as experimental data. It is perhaps for this reason that "dressing for the part" has as far as possible been avoided. The young men and women who build the houses and plow the fields and form the pottery wear the same overalls, sweaters, and rubber boots as farmers and factory workers anywhere else—to the disappointment of visitors, who have complained because dye plants are shredded in an ordinary mincing machine and boiled in an ordinary casserole, or because the pottery makers work at ordinary deal tables and use electric light. But "authenticity"—or at least apparent authenticity—is not the aim of the experimental center. Ten years of experiment in Iron Age metallurgy would be necessary (and is going on) before a genuine reproduction of an Iron Age caldron could be made by Iron Age methods, and even then it would be fantastically expensive to produce. And it would give exactly the same results as a modern iron pot. Some watchfulness is required to prevent the center from becoming a sort of prehistoric Disneyland. The public may view the experiments; it may not influence them. But the public is not ignored, and side by side with its experimental work the center has developed an educational organization.

It began with television. After the first experimental houses were built, Denmark's radio station and Hans-Ole Hansen together produced a series of documentary films and programs designed for the schools' television service. These films resulted in a growing demand from enterprising history teachers that their classes should be allowed to visit this living bit of prehistoric Denmark. In due course a comprehensive program for school history classes was built up, beginning with one-day tours, where the children have the thrill of scrambling around the Iron Age village, eating their box lunches around the hearth of one of the houses, and perhaps helping to rake out the ashes from a pottery-firing pit to expose the nest of "Iron Age" vessels within. Older children are allowed to camp for a week at a time in the neighborhood and take part in the work of the center. There is a lake, and on the wooded shore an area has been set aside for experimental reconstruction of Stone Age houses. All the actual work of preparing the timber, weaving the wattles, building the walls, and thatching the roofs is done by schoolchildren, under the supervision of the center's staff.

Now again the work of the various departments began to impinge on one another. The weaving and pottery laboratories began to find a market for their products in the schools, which

wanted "authentic" specimens of prehistoric handicrafts that were still not so irreplaceable that they could not be handled and used by the pupils. Museums began commissioning exact copies of some of their best and most fragile textiles, which could not be risked on traveling exhibitions. Another venture also proved profitable. Experiments had for some time been going on in the production of "monk-stones," the large red bricks of various architectural shapes with which medieval Danish churches had been built. And now requests began to come in from parish councils throughout the country for bricks to be used in repair and restoration.

But first and foremost, and in rapidly increasing numbers, have come the tourists. The enthusiastic tales of the schoolchildren, and the television programs and newspaper articles, have brought Danes to the center by the thousands. The visitors to Lejre experience the impact of prehistory brought alive. This is how Denmark had been, not in a model or in a film or behind the glass cases of museums, but to be lived and felt and experienced. You gather handfuls of raspberries in the bushes that border the cultivated clearing, discuss with the "inhabitants" the state of the crops in the neat little fields, dry your clothes after a rainstorm by the glowing hearth of the long house while the loom clacks in the background, or take a turn with the rubbingstone on the saddle quern beside the grain bin. You are on a visit to your ancestors of two thousand years ago, and the gap of the centuries has somehow become meaningless.

The research center at Lejre has, without intending it, become an experiment with Time itself.

One of HORIZON'S *most distinguished reporters on ancient life, Geoffrey Bibby is as much at home in prehistoric Europe (see "The Body in the Bog," Winter, 1968) as he is in the Near East (see "Looking for Dilmun," Autumn, 1969).*

ARCHAEOLOGICAL RESEARCH CENTER, LEJRE

These researchers are wearing reproductions of their ancestors' cloaks and caps. The copies are based on chemical and other analyses of ancient fabrics and are so accurate as to be indistinguishable from the originals.

Montaigne's Soul Mate

There is nothing like life in a dank château to promote, in a growing girl, a taste for literature

We grieve for many; not least we grieve for unhappy, solitary maidens so intelligent as to be misfits in ordinary life. We grieve for the superior among inferiors. We grieve for Marie le Jars de Gournay, the "adoptive daughter" of Michel de Montaigne.

Marie le Jars was born in Paris in 1565, the eldest child of a noble gentleman and officeholder. He bought, out of pride, the moated, towered, and turreted manor of Gournay, fifty miles northeast of Paris; and he died in 1577. His widow, left with very little cash and with six children to be established and dowered, abandoned Paris for the economical gloom of Gournay; from it Marie took her name.

There is nothing like life in a dank château to promote, in a growing girl, a taste for literature. Having no proper teacher, Marie taught herself Latin by comparing the original texts with French translations. (That fine linguist, George Borrow, later learned strange tongues by the same method.) She even made some progress in Greek. She read whatever she could find, defiant of her mother, who regarded such occupations as perverse. She was an alarming girl, who chilled the parents of eligible young gentlemen. It was determined that two of her sisters should be married off and one consigned to a convent, while Marie must rub along as best she could. She was not ill-looking; she was of medium height, with a good figure, chestnut hair, a round face neither beautiful nor ugly, she says. But she was brusque in manner, subject to fits of violent anger, and given to unladylike outrightness of speech. She could see no promise of happiness and little meaning in life.

Many a life has been shaped by the discovery of a book. Into Marie's ken came, somehow, a copy of Montaigne's *Essays* (1580). The reading of the book was a lightning shock, a portent, a mystical experience. Montaigne, that kindly, skeptical, middle-aged gentleman in his book-lined tower near Bordeaux, would seem no soul mate for an adolescent girl; but he taught that each of us is a worthy subject for study. Examining himself, he revealed Marie. His book was to her sacred, inerrant, its author only a little less than a god.

Early in 1588 Montaigne came to Paris on a confidential mission for King Henry of Navarre, and also to see a second edition of the *Essays* through the press. Shortly after his arrival Marie and her mother visited Paris on family business. When Marie learned that her spiritual kinsman had transferred his physical presence to her neighborhood, she recognized the kindly purpose of fate. She wrote him a fan letter that must have been a triumph of the genre. She gave evidence of her total immersion in Montaigne's thought and style; she offered discipleship and adoration. No author, however cynical about human behavior, is proof against such appreciation. Immediately Montaigne called on Marie, and if we are to believe her, on that very day he termed her his *fille d'alliance*, his daughter by adoption. No doubt he uttered the words humorously, but Marie was never responsive to humor, and least of all at that sacred moment. Thenceforth she called him *mon père* and demanded, in all her writings, recognition of her daughtership.

Montaigne was now fifty-five and in poor health. His book had been well received, but it had never evoked such passionate enthusiasm as Marie displayed. He was touched; he had not had much affection from his own chilly daughter. He was readily persuaded to pay long visits to the château. There he could talk at his ease of art and philosophy and of the new edition of his book, of which he had the proofs in pocket. Some important additions to the manuscript are in her handwriting; they must have been written to her adoptive father's dictation. It was an affectionate collaboration. But Montaigne essayed no union of the flesh; that would have been incestuous.

Authorship is contagious, the literary itch is allayed by pen-scratching. One day, on a country walk, Marie told an endless romantic tale of parted lovers, a borrowed tale, in fact. "Splendid! You must write it down!" said Montaigne, though with how much conviction it is hard to say. She wrote it down, entitled it *Le Proumenoir de M. de Montaigne*, or *A Walk with Montaigne*, and in time sent it to him at his southern house. He did not reply. Perhaps he was too ill; perhaps he could not think what to say. Those few indomitable scholars who have read it have found it woefully dull, its one merit a plea for women's education to save them from sentimental disaster.

Montaigne left Paris for Bordeaux in November, 1588, and Marie's year of bliss ended. In 1591 her mother died, and upon Marie, the eldest child, fell the duty of settling the estate, which was all too inadequate for the family needs. The Gournay château was left to a brother, and she retired to modest quarters in Paris. There she learned, early in 1593, of Montaigne's death. Inevitably, she was prostrated with grief.

Montaigne, who was an incessant reviser of his own work and patcher-in of afterthoughts, left a mass of marginal notes in view of a new edition. His widow sent a copy of the manuscript to Marie in Paris, with the request that she edit the text and supervise the printing of a new edition. This Marie did with evident competence, although some critics have ascribed to her own pen certain passages in which the master praises the disciple with unlikely fulsomeness. In any case she read the proofs, filled lacunae, translated

By MORRIS BISHOP

quotations, and provided a rather finical introduction. She defied all critics, all criticism. "All is perfect in this book," she wrote. "The gods and goddesses gave him their language."

After a year's visit with Montaigne's widow and daughter in Périgord, Marie settled down to lead the literary life in Paris. The period was a barren one for literature. Marie's income could barely support her with decency. She frequented the salon of Marguerite de Valois, divorced wife of King Henry IV, and from her received a small pension. She aimed higher, at the king himself, although he was reported never to have read a book in his life. She addressed to him an essay on the education of princes, and an ecstatic poem in which she alleged that she would gladly drown in his bath water. She was presented to the gallant monarch in 1610, and a month later he was assassinated. The knife that slew him severed all Marie's hopes.

Nine-year-old Louis XIII succeeded his father; before long effective power over France was wielded by Cardinal Richelieu, who piqued himself on his literary taste and enjoyed distributing scholarly patronage. He received Marie jocosely, greeting her with a string of archaisms in the style of Montaigne. He was surprised and little abashed by the dignity of her response. He said to his literary agent, Boisrobert: "We must do something for Mademoiselle de Gournay. I'll give her a pension of two hundred crowns." "She has a companion, Mademoiselle Jamyn, daughter of the poet Ronsard's page," said Boisrobert. "All right, I'll give the companion fifty francs a year." "Then there's her cat, my darling Piaillon." "Twenty francs a year for the cat; she shall live on tripe," said the cardinal. "And the cat has kittened," said Boisrobert. "Oh, very well; one pistole apiece for the kittens."

Heartened by her pension, Marie established a salon in her attic quarters on the rue de l'Arbre. To reach them, visitors made the last stage of their ascent by a steep spiral stair with

Marie de Gournay

a rope for guardrail. Here, we are told, the scheme for the Académie Française originated, but with the encouragement of the Cardinal it found a more accessible home elsewhere.

The chilly apartment was a public-relations office, designed to spread Montaigne's fame and influence. Several editions of the *Essays* issued thence. Marie also carried on an endless battle in defense of sixteenth-century poets, especially Ronsard, against the restrictive critical principles and practices of the new school. She demanded freedom, richness, frenzy, in imaginative literature; she scorned the tendency toward purity and correctness, which, she thought, would end only in making French a dead language.

Constantly she wrote. Her published works run to well over a thousand printed pages. But her poetry is flat, her polemics so out-of-date as to be nearly meaningless. The chief interest of her work lies in its feminism, its protest against women's subordination to men, its insistence on the equality of the sexes, its demand for decent education for women.

She grew old, thin, and ugly. To defray the costs of the literary life, she made unrewarding experiments with alchemy. She was hailed as the French Minerva, the tenth Muse, the siren of France. She accepted the tributes graciously, ignoring the covert snigger. She had a set of false teeth made of walrus ivory. As these did not fit very well, she removed them to eat and adroitly reinserted them to talk. Her pronouncements were much quoted. Asked if she thought pederasty a crime,

she replied: "God forbid that I should condemn what Socrates practiced."

Heartless practical jokers, male, made her their victim. On one occasion Mademoiselle de Gournay sent a copy of her collected works to the poet Racan, whom she admired without having the pleasure of his acquaintance. Learning that Racan proposed to thank the authoress in person, a noble farceur called a little before the appointed hour, presented himself as Racan, and overwhelmed the poor lady with extravagant compliments. As soon as he left a second comedian appeared, asserting that he was the real Racan and that the first was a conscienceless impostor. Then the genuine Racan climbed the stairs; he was greeted, according to one version, by a shower of slippers. The story, variously embellished, had a great success; Boisrobert, Cardinal Richelieu's familiar, made a play of it.

Such practical jokes, cruel as they were to the proud old lady, were less malevolent than most lethal jests of the period. Marie, the grotesque old maid with her pretensions and out-of-date enthusiasms, was ordained to be a butt. However, she bore the mockeries with dignity and often confounded the mockers. The scurrilous Tallemant des Réaux admits she never forgot a kindness. Another writer, Michel de Marolles, visited her nearly every day and regarded her with almost filial affection.

She was a gallant figure, confronting age and decrepitude with high spirit. Until the end (at the age of eighty) she fought for worthy causes: beautiful letters, the intellectual liberation of women, the fame of her adopted father, Montaigne. She was indeed absurd in the eyes of her contemporaries. Now her contemporaries have themselves a look of absurdity. And not her contemporaries only. . . .

This is the fifth in a series of biographical escapades by Morris Bishop. A collection of short biographies by Professor Bishop, The Exotics, *was published last fall by American Heritage Press.*

THE LAST OF
THE DESERT ADVENTURERS

Forty years of ceaseless roaming in Africa, Arabia, and Asia has
established him as the outstanding traveler of his age. Thesiger is
a name in company with Sir Richard Burton and T. E. Lawrence

The fading snapshots pasted neatly into the family album appear to show an Edwardian picnic. There is a well-pitched tent, a clutter of deck chairs and folding tables, ladies in long, high-waisted dresses. But look closer. The ground is arid and dusty, the branches on the few trees strut out horizontal with the ground, and the little eighteen-month-old boy who trots happily among the guy ropes or sits upright on a mule wears a pith helmet in addition to his white shirt and shorts. A string of camels stand idly in the background. Turn the page and there is another snapshot of the same small boy, now three years old, his head still shrouded in that enormous pith helmet, clutching a rifle in his hand, a dead oryx at his feet. These are not pictures of lazy picnics at Eton on the Fourth of June or an idle afternoon out hunting rabbits in the meadow. This is Ethiopia in all its primitive splendor—and harshness—in the days just before the First World War. A country still locked almost as deeply in the Middle Ages as it had been in the 1790's, when the Scottish adventurer James Bruce penetrated to its interior in search of the source of the Blue Nile and returned with tales, often unbelieved, of people who ate living meat, of flogging, mutilation, and summary execution by a variety of brutal methods. Yet it was also a country of great beauty where lion and gazelle and buffalo roamed

free and the people were quite untouched by the advance of civilization. The capital, Addis Ababa, was still to be reached only by a long, hard journey on foot or by mule over the four hundred miles from the Red Sea coast.

It was over this tortuous route that the Honorable Wilfred Thesiger, newly appointed British minister to Addis Ababa, brought his young wife, Kathleen Mary, in the late autumn of 1909. They set up a home in the British legation that consisted simply of an interconnecting series of circular grass-roofed huts. And there, on June 3, 1910, Mrs. Thesiger gave birth to a son whom they christened Wilfred Patrick. He was the first Englishman ever born in Ethiopia.

This is the child in the snapshots, who grew up knowing only the wide horizons of Ethiopia. When he was eight months old, he was carried for three weeks in a swaying litter between two mules to the railhead at Dire Dawa as his family set out on home leave. A few months later he was carried back over the same rugged course. The water for his food on these treks had to be boiled and then strained through gamgee tissue.

Looking at these snapshots now with the tall, craggy man who is guiding one through the pages, it is hard to picture him as that child. Yet, as Wilfred Thesiger, ensconced in the small, monastically simple room he maintains

in his mother's London flat, speaks of it all with deep nostalgia, one can see that he is reaching back into the past to savor those childhood days. And it becomes easier to understand how he emerged from this Ethiopian childhood to become an explorer—and a big-game hunter—almost without equal in his generation. Nearly forty years of almost ceaseless roaming in Africa, Arabia, and Asia has established him as the outstanding traveler of his age. Thesiger is a name in company with Sir Richard Burton, Charles Doughty, Bertram Thomas, and T. E. Lawrence.

He has been awarded the Founder's Medal by the Royal Geographical Society, the Lawrence of Arabia Medal by the Royal Central Asian Society, and the Livingstone Medal by the Royal Scottish Geographical Society. Sir John Glubb, former commander of the Arab Legion, once wrote, "Wilfred Thesiger is perhaps the last, and certainly one of the greatest, of British travelers among the Arabs." The *London Sunday Times* put it more succinctly: "He is our greatest living explorer."

His two books *Arabian Sands* and *Marsh Arabs* are classics among travel literature; *Arabian Sands*, in particular, which tells of his two journeys on foot and camel across the Empty Quarter of Arabia, charts not only the adventure but the developing mind of the adventurer. Thesiger seeks to explain what it is that draws him back again

By TIMOTHY S. GREEN

Wilfred Thesiger, perhaps the last man to explore uncharted terrain on this planet, on his second crossing of Arabia's Empty Quarter, in 1947

and again to pit himself against the harsh desert life, where one is constantly threatened by heat, thirst, hunger, and unknown raiders.

"The Empty Quarter," he wrote, "offered me the chance to win distinction as a traveler; but I believed that it could give me more than this, that in those empty wastes I could find the peace that comes with solitude, and, among the Bedu, comradeship in a hostile world."

There is inherent in Thesiger's nature a fierce determination to live life stripped right down to bedrock, challenging the rawest forces of nature on their own terms. As a traveler, as a hunter, even as a soldier, Thesiger gave no quarter—and didn't expect to be given any himself. When he went after a lion, he tracked it on foot for hours across the hot plains of the Sudan, matching his hunting skill and endurance against the lion's until he caught up with it. Then it was Thesiger and

the lion facing each other squarely. "I've been charged sixteen times by lions. I was convinced that I would eventually be killed by one—I didn't think my luck could hold."

Thesiger's passion for the desert and his rather idealized view of primitive life have bred in him not only a great resistance to change but a far-reaching disillusionment with the human race. "We are like dinosaurs—the last of a dying race. In the past, man—ever since he ceased to be an ape—succeeded because he was more adaptable than any other animal. Now the human race is rapidly becoming specialized, as dependent on its urban environment as the gorilla is on the forest. The new technological civilization that we have evolved destroys or corrupts every culture with which it comes into contact. Cultures and civilizations that have gone on for thousands of years are disappearing like snow on the lawn in a hot sun."

Thesiger's life has been an unceasing search for those last pockets of humanity forgotten or bypassed in the rush of the twentieth century. Walking, always walking, he has ferreted out those havens of tranquillity far from the madding car. His own estimate is that he has walked more than forty thousand miles. When persistent pain in his knees forced him to have a cartilage operation in 1967, the surgeon told him afterward, "You've simply worn out your knee joints with walking." Within months of the operation he was back walking as unflaggingly as ever.

Thesiger's father, the Honorable Wilfred Thesiger, led a wandering life as a diplomat. By birth he was an aristocrat; his brother Viscount Chelmsford was viceroy of India. He arrived in Addis Ababa just as Ethiopia was plunging into a civil war that would last for seven years, until 1916, when a coup engineered by Ras Tafari Makonnen (now the emperor Haile Selassie) at last brought peace to the country. During the struggle Mr. Thesiger sheltered Ras Tafari's oldest son in the British legation—an action that earned the Thesiger family the lifelong gratitude of the present emperor. For young Wilfred, growing up amid such turmoil was like *King Solomon's Mines* or other stories of Rider Haggard, which his father often read to him in the evenings, come to life.

Apart from his three younger brothers, Wilfred saw nothing of other European boys of his own age. Life in the legation was essentially an adult life into which the children fitted as best they could. They rode before breakfast, had a few lessons, drilled with the legation's soldiers (including joining them in pigsticking with lances), did a few more lessons, then had lunch. The afternoons were devoted mostly to riding with their own escort of lancers.

It was a world so adult, so aristocratic, so unlike anything most English boys experienced, that to be removed from it suddenly and pitched into the narrow, disciplined world of a private school was like stepping from a palace into a prison. In 1919 the Thesiger family returned to England, and Wilfred was sent to private school. During his first term in this new, totally alien environment he suffered the added shock of the death of his father, who was only forty-seven. His mother was left to bring up four rather unruly boys, all under ten years of age.

Young Wilfred's world seemed to collapse around him. He clutched at memories. As his teachers droned on in the cold classrooms, his mind drifted back to the heat, the dust, the smells of Ethiopia, building a lasting romantic legend around his image of that country.

Eton, to which he was transferred when he was thirteen, was not much happier. He did not get on with his classical tutor, his studies were erratic, and he was intolerant of the authority of senior boys. His greatest pleasure during his Eton and later his Oxford years was the holidays spent at a large

COLL. OF MRS. R. ASTLEY THESIGER

An ambassador's sons at "home," Wilfred (at left) and his brother Brian hunt in Ethiopia.

country house, The Milebrook, that his mother had leased on the Stanage estate on the border of Wales. In this open countryside Wilfred led his brothers on endless walks over the hills in search of ravens' and peregrines' nests. The Stanage estate was one of the best pheasant ranges in England, and he was often invited to shoot there. He had been given his first gun, a double-barreled .410, when he was seven. By now he was a good shot and took his shooting very seriously. If the boys were invited to a party in the evening, he would drag his brothers home early, saying, "we must get to bed early to keep our eye in."

Yet that rolling border country was only a substitute for the Africa that filled his dreams. His chance to return came in 1930. As his father's heir he was invited to attend Haile Selassie's coronation. As he stepped off the train in Addis Ababa (the railway had by this time penetrated from the coast), the mantle that had shrouded his life for twelve years was suddenly cast away. He wrote to a friend in England, "It has all come back and it almost seems as if I had never been away."

Once in Ethiopia he began to scheme to get away into the wilds. He asked Colonel R. E. Cheesman, the explorer of the Blue Nile, who lived in Addis Ababa, what corners of Ethiopia were as yet unexplored. Cheesman suggested that no one had ever tracked the Awash River, which ran through the dangerous Dankali country east of Addis Ababa toward French Somaliland. The Danakil had a reputation for collecting the testicles of their enemies, and few white men had ever returned alive from that desolate country. This was exactly the challenge Thesiger sought. He had no time to mount a full expedition because he had to return to Oxford, but he trekked down to take a preliminary look at the fringes of the country. Thesiger has always said since, that this four-week journey "was the most decisive month in my life."

By the autumn of 1933 he was back in Addis Ababa ready to go. The government, however, was reluctant to let him start because there was constant fighting between the tribes in the Dankali country. Final permission was granted only after weeks of arguing. He wrote home, "I should have been a broken man if they had refused me."

It was a remarkable journey. Thesiger was not yet twenty-four, and he had little experience of trekking through desert, negotiating with potentially hostile tribes, or handling a retinue of thirty-eight armed men. Undeterred, he led his men slowly north along the Awash River to the border of the Aussa Sultanate. Here, after discussions lasting half the night with the local sultan, who was surrounded by an imposing array of four hundred armed Danakil, Thesiger won permission to track the river through the sultanate. After weeks of travel he followed the Awash to its end in a lonely salt lake, thus solving the mystery of where this river, which rises on the plains near Addis Ababa, finally vanishes. The importance of the expedition was noted by the Royal Geographical Society, which invited Thesiger to deliver a paper on his exploits.

Thesiger was already casting about for an opening that might offer him a springboard to adventure. He found it in the Sudan Political Service, which he joined in January, 1935. He was posted to Darfur Province to work with the district commissioner, Guy Moore. They were the only Englishmen in a territory of fifty thousand square miles. Moore had served previously as a political officer in Iraq and had acquired a great attachment for the Arab people. He was to change Thesiger's whole attitude toward travel. For all his enthusiasm, Thesiger had up to that point really seen nothing but Ethiopia, and he had traveled very much as a European, complete with tent, servants, and tinned food. Guy Moore altered all that. "He explained the life of the desert and the Arab to me. On trek he always lived on native food and didn't care if he didn't eat for twenty-four hours. He fed with the local chiefs, sitting with them on the floor—not aloof on a chair like most of the district commissioners. Like this, one had a sense of common humanity with them."

In the Sudan Thesiger began riding camels for the first time. He spent every spare penny on six of the best riding camels he could find, and on these he learned to travel long, hard, and fast, carrying few supplies beyond a bag of dates and a little flour.

His other great passion in the Sudan was big-game hunting. During his years in the political service he killed a total of seventy lions, tracking them down on foot or galloping them down on horseback. Among his friends his lion-hunting feats became legendary. "He was so tough," one of them recalls, "that he simply ran after the lion until it gave in from sheer exhaustion. He could outrun it."

The threat of war put a temporary end to his desert journeys and big-game hunting, but he threw himself into new exploits with equal passion. The conquest of Ethiopia by the Italians in 1936 and the enforced exile of his old friend Haile Selassie had disturbed him deeply. "It was the one great emotional cause of my life. This was my home, the country of my childhood being raped—and England did nothing. It was heartbreaking."

Thesiger dedicated Arabian Sands *to his two Bedu friends bin Kabina and bin Ghabaisha.*

In 1940 came the chance to redeem past omissions. Thesiger was invited to join the Sudan Defense Force, which was getting ready to invade Ethiopia to reinstate the emperor. He helped organize the local patriot forces to support the invasion force that was gathering on the plains of the Sudan. It was a role aptly suited to his temperament: no worries about paper work, just fast traveling through rough country and living off the land. When the main invasion force advanced, he ranged ahead through the mountains, cajoling the local chiefs into harassing the fleeing Italians. The campaign was exhausting and frequently frustrating, for many of the Ethiopian leaders were unpredictable and might switch their loyalties over some petty jealousy. But these trials could not diminish Thesiger's feeling of triumph at having helped restore Haile Selassie to his throne. "The whole campaign," he said with pride, "was a personal crusade." For his role in it he was awarded the D.S.O.

Then, with barely a pause for breath, Thesiger was posted to Syria and found himself thrust, for the first time, into the world of the Arab. He was captivated. "It was the first time I had heard Arabic spoken as a native language and I realized at once what a beautiful language it is. Then too I

met with the open hospitality and courtesy of the Arab. I liked their pride of race, their tradition—I had a feeling of the past. But just as he was becoming deeply involved, he was transferred to another assignment in North Africa, one that occupied his attention for much of the time until the end of the war. Not until late in 1945 did he have further opportunity to live among the Arabs.

As he stood on the brink of the Arabian sands, he was just thirty-five years old: a tall, yet very spare man with a tight, tense face and a Roman nose that jutted out like some bleak rock in the desert. A man of strange moods and contrasts, he could be affable and charming one second, then suddenly as remote as if he had withdrawn from this planet in all but his physical presence.

The actual excuse that was to take him to Arabia was an assignment from the Middle East Anti-Locust Unit to try to pinpoint the breeding grounds in southern Arabia of the swarms of locusts that from time to time came marauding on the desert wind to devastate huge areas of the Middle East.

Even in 1946 only a handful of Europeans had penetrated far into the million square miles of desert in Arabia. Sir Richard Burton had made his secret pilgrimage to Mecca in 1853, Charles Doughty had spent two years (1876–78) wandering in the western deserts. But it was not until the 1930's that two men successfully spanned the great waste of sand that sweeps almost nine hundred miles southeast from the Persian Gulf to Yemen. The Arabs call it Rub al Khali, the Empty Quarter. Bertram Thomas was the first to make a full crossing of these sands, in 1931; Harry St. John Philby followed in 1932. Thesiger was to become the third man. The fact that he was not the first to cross did not make it any easier; the physical and mental challenge presented by the desert was just as great.

"The air was like a flame in the sun," Doughty had written, "the sand was as

Crossing the Empty Quarter, a trip from which the Bedu shrink, Thesiger's party slowly descends a great dune. In the Empty Quarter the dunes reach heights of several hundred feet.

burning coals beneath my feet." But the struggle to survive brought its rewards. "Though your mouth glows, and your skin is parched," wrote Burton, "yet you feel no languor, the effect of humid heat; your lungs are lightened, your spirit brightens, your memory recovers its tone, and your spirits become exuberant; your fancy and imagination are powerfully aroused, and the wilderness and sublimity of the scenes around you stir up all the energies of your soul—whether for exertion, danger or strife. Your *morale* improves; you become frank and cordial, hospitable and single-minded; the hypocritical politeness and the slavery of civilization are left behind you in the city. Your senses are quickened; they require no stimulants but air and exercise, in the Desert spirituous liquors excite only disgust. There is keen enjoyment of mere animal existence."

Thesiger's own growing appreciation of both the desert and the Arabs was compounded by studying such accounts. But this did not immediately endow him with a passport to the Empty Quarter. He had to serve an apprenticeship on the fringes of the desert, getting to know the Bedu, coming to grips with their language, trying to grasp their way of life and at the same time win their acceptance.

His most constant companions during his first five months in Arabia in the winter of 1945–46 were men from the Bait Kathir and Rashid tribes. One of them, Salim bin Kabina of the Rashid, was to remain a close friend throughout the five years Thesiger spent in Arabia; another young Rashid, Salim bin Ghabaisha, was to join the entourage the following winter for the first crossing of the Empty Quarter. There is a splendid photograph of these two in *Arabian Sands* (see page 107), perched atop some desert crag, rifles slung carelessly over their shoulders, broad, curved daggers thrust into wide belts that also bristled with cartridges, their lean, hard bodies, clothed in worn jelabahs, their long, slightly hawklike faces fringed by shoulder-length tangles of black hair. Though many of the Arabs may have treated Thesiger with some reserve, these two looked up to him as some wise patron, and it was through their friendship that Thesiger was able to break the crust of Bedu suspicion and come to grips with the harsh reality of the lives of these people. Sixteen-year-old bin Kabina had been on the very brink of disaster when he first met Thesiger. His one and only camel had died. "I wept as I sat there in the dark beside the body of my old grey camel," he told Thesiger. "She was old, long past bearing, and she was very thin for there was no rain in the desert for a long time; but she was my camel. The only one we had. That night, Umbarak ["blessed one," as the Arabs called Thesiger], death seemed very close to me and my family." Then he added cheerfully: "God brought you. Now I shall have everything."

That first winter Thesiger's journeys were fairly limited. He traveled through the rocky mountain terrain to the south of the Empty Quarter and on the fringe of the sands. The summer of 1946, spent back in England, was one long bout of anticipation for the great journey to come, for now he was ready for the real open desert. He returned to Salala, on the southern coast of Arabia, in October, 1946, to attack the Empty Quarter.

The round trip he proposed from Salala, on the Indian Ocean, to the Liwa Oasis, just inland from the Persian Gulf, was two thousand miles long. He hoped to complete it in three months. On this odyssey his clothes, equipment, and supplies were stripped down to the bare minimum. He wore only a colored loincloth and a long shirt, although he did permit himself a sleeping bag for protection against the bitter desert nights. He normally went barefoot. His men received a ration of three-quarters of a pound of flour daily; they also took rice, butter, coffee, tea, sugar, and a few dates. Their menu over the long weeks of the journey hardly varied except for the occasional luxury of a goat, a gazelle, or a desert hare.

The priority at all times was to get to the next well, with its brackish water that even the camels were often reluctant to drink. For Thesiger the endless march over sand dunes in the burning heat of the day seemed to sap his lifeblood. "The sun was scorching hot and I felt empty, sick, and dizzy," he wrote in *Arabian Sands*. "As I struggled up the slope knee deep in shifting sand, my heart thumped wildly and my thirst grew worse. I found it difficult to swallow; even my ears felt blocked, and yet I knew that it would be many intolerable hours before I could drink."

The longest single haul over the heart of the sands took fourteen days.

Thesiger and his four companions and their camels reached the point of exhaustion. They approached each new dune in despair of ever reaching the top. Their water supply was reduced to foul-tasting dregs in the goatskin bags; the daily ration of hard, dry bread stuck in their mouths. Apart from a few drops of coffee when they arose in the bitter cold before dawn, they marched all day with practically nothing to eat or drink, only moistening their lips occasionally. Once a small hare scuttered across their path and gave them a few scraps of meat for some soup. For the Bedu this was a part of their normal way of life—although many of them hesitated at the thought of crossing the sands. As for Thesiger, he was carried onward by sheer determination, perhaps even excitement. After all, the Empty Quarter was the Mount Everest or the South Pole of desert travel: the ultimate goal.

And what was the reward at the end of it? "It was a personal experience, and the reward had been a drink of clean, nearly tasteless water. I was content with that."

The actual crossing of the sands to the Liwa Oasis, where Thesiger had to remain discreetly out of sight in the dunes because the Saudi Arabians were hostile to any Christian venturing far into the desert, was hardly half the journey. They now turned east toward Oman and began the long swing back to Salala. This proved in some ways the trickiest part of the trip. Although the challenges of sun and sand were not so intense and there were more wells, they were desperately short of food. For more than a month they ate no meat.

There was an additional danger in passing through the territory of several fanatically anti-Christian tribes in Oman. Word of Thesiger's exploits the previous year on the fringe of the sands had filtered through. Some Bedu were determined that the Christian must not pass through their domain if he returned.

Despite these threats, Thesiger was in no hurry to return to Salala. He was not eager for the journey to end. Where possible he and his companions moved at a leisurely pace. He had slipped into the rhythm of the nomadic Arab, drifting along with no deadline to be anywhere—provided the waterskins were full. He saw the Bedu in their natural setting, virtually untouched as yet by the outside world. He listened by the hour to their endless chatter about this raid or that man's violent death, often hearing, as he sipped his coffee, the same story over and over again. It could be tedious, it could be irritating, but he was assimilating both their life and their legends. He came to know their individual problems, their triumphs, and their weaknesses. And all the while his admiration for the basic nobility of the desert Arab grew. "When I came to write my book, I wanted it to be a tribute to the Bedu, a tribute to what the spirit of man can achieve under these hard conditions if left to himself."

Yet for all his high regard for the desert Arabs and his surrender to their way of life, Thesiger retained his detachment. He was with them and accepted by them, but was not of them. When he and his companions finally emerged from the desert after the first crossing of the Empty Quarter, he luxuriated in the chance to speak English again, to bathe, to eat substantial hot food, and to relax in a chair instead of squatting on the ground.

These differences enhance the appeal of the desert for him. He has never set out to live the rest of his life there. He thrives on contrast. After three months of sheer struggle to stay alive, he savors the pleasures of civilization all the more, yet he is sustained also by the knowledge that he will return to the desert.

The first crossing of the Empty Quarter served to sharpen his appetite. He was anxious to test himself against it again and to satisfy his curiosity about the little known area of the western sands. The Anti-Locust Unit, to whom he had sent a report on his first journey, was prepared to keep him on in Arabia, but not in the western sands, where there were no locusts. So he made a bold decision to stand on his own and finance his future Arabian travels himself.

During the second crossing of the Empty Quarter, in the winter of 1947-48, there was one sharp reminder that the Arabia he had grown to love was changing. As he squatted with his Bedu companions around the campfire one night after crossing the sands, the desert sky in the distance was illuminated by headlights, and he heard the roar of a car engine as it struggled across the sand. It was an omen for the future of Arabia—and one that he cursed. Actually, the car was carrying none other than St. John Philby, who had crossed the Empty Quarter before Thesiger in the early 1930's and who was now living in Saudi Arabia as adviser to King Ibn Saud.

Although the physical hardships of the second crossing were not as trying as those of the previous year, the danger from Bedu tribes was far greater. The desert was in a state of war; large raiding parties were on the move. Word traveled around the tribes that the Christian was daring to venture into the sands again. At least one party set out to intercept and kill him. Moreover Thesiger's expedition was defying King Ibn Saud by exploring the western areas of the sands. They were on constant alert, their rifles never out of their hands. One cold, wet night their camels were frightened by a movement in the darkness of the dunes. Were raiders about to attack? The expedition members stayed awake all night staring into the gloom, only to find in the morning the tracks of a wolf that had circled the camp.

Finally, when they were safely across the sands and came to a well near Sulaiyil to water their camels, their luck seemed to run out. Thesiger and his four companions were arrested by local officials, who then sent messages to Ibn Saud asking what should be done to the infidel who had come illegally into their midst. Two anxious days followed. Thesiger pleaded that he alone was responsible and asked that his companions be freed. But he feared some reprisal against them as a lesson to other Bedu not to lead Christians into forbidden territory. Finally word came from Ibn Saud that Thesiger and his party could go free. St. John Philby had interceded with the king and obtained their release.

Thesiger pressed north to the Laila Oasis, then turned east toward the Trucial States, a clutch of tiny sheikdoms on the shores of the Persian Gulf. Unlike the first year, he did not return through Saudi Arabia and Oman to the East Aden Protectorate, but lingered on the Trucial Coast, at that point quite untouched by the invasions of oilmen who were to change it so drastically fifteen years later.

Thesiger spent the next two winters on the coast and on forays into Oman. Much of the time he posed as an Arab from the north to avoid the genuine hostility to any Christian. Although these years were rewarding, they were something of an anticlimax after the two great journeys across the Empty Quarter. Always at the back of Thesiger's mind was the bitter knowledge that his field of operations was becoming more and more cramped. He defied a ban by the sultan of Muscat forbidding him to enter his land, but such a challenge to authority could not be allowed to pass unnoticed. In the winter of 1949, when he set out to continue exploration of the Jabal al Akhadar mountains in the east of Oman, he was stopped by a hundred armed tribesmen who told him they had orders from the imam of Oman to kill him unless he turned back. He suspected they might shoot him anyway simply to claim the reward money, but he managed to arrange a safe-conduct with a local sheik.

This armed intervention finally made it clear that the time had come to leave Arabia. A complete chapter, indeed the most significant chapter, of his life

was at an end. The final words of *Arabian Sands* are, "I knew how it felt to go into exile."

When Thesiger came to write about his Arabian journeys, he chose to do it in Copenhagen. His reason: the bleak climate of that northern city was in total contrast to his Arabian experiences. "If I had written the book in Morocco or Greece," he explains, "I would have described the sun as I saw it outside the window there; I would have described the desert as I saw it in Morocco. Copenhagen in the rain was so different I had to relive the journeys."

The book was published, to universal acclaim, nine years after Thesiger bade farewell to Arabia. Although he had wandered widely in the intervening years, he had found only one other unspoiled corner of the Middle East that could offer him any lasting substitute for the desert—the marshes of southern Iraq between the Euphrates and the Tigris. He went there for several months every year from 1950 until the summer of 1958—and in duration, if not in emotion, this love affair with the marshes was greater than the one with the desert. The two existences could hardly have been more different. In the desert he had undertaken long and arduous journeys with a handful of companions, matching himself against the elements. In the marshes there were no great journeys to undertake; instead he became much more a part of the community of the marshmen. He shared with those simple, illiterate Arabs their precarious existence in a world of endless lagoons, where island villages could be swamped by a heavy rainfall. He found much to admire in their customs, which had evolved so slowly over the centuries and had not yet been touched by the onrush of civilization. The huge cathedral-like *mudhifs*, guest houses made of reeds, with bundles of long reeds forming stout buttresses and pillars, seemed to him much greater architectural achievements than any modern edifice of steel

and concrete. Indeed, one of his biggest regrets at the changes that must inevitably penetrate the marshes was that this art, built up over perhaps two thousand years, would vanish overnight.

For the moment, however, the marshes were unspoiled; few of the marshmen had gone off to be "corner boys" in Bagdad. Thesiger moved through the watery lanes in a long slim canoe called a *tarada*, his medicine chest and rifle by his side. "I spent those years in the Marshes because I enjoyed being there," he wrote in his second book, *Marsh Arabs*. "I thought of it as home."

His self-taught medical skill made him welcome, and appreciating this point, he took it seriously. On his brief visits to London he consulted doctors about surgical techniques and the best drugs with which to stock his medicine chest. It worked to the advantage of both sides: the Arabs got their medicine, and Thesiger earned the acceptance that enabled him to live in their villages and do what he wanted.

The late Gavin Maxwell, the travel writer, made one journey into the marshes with Thesiger and in his book *A Reed Shaken by the Wind* described Thesiger at work. "For nearly three hours," wrote Maxwell, "Thesiger worked indefatigably in the midst of this bedlam; his hypodermic stabbed with piston-like regularity at brown bottoms; oceans of ointment were spread on leagues of lint; he stitched away like a tailor at dog bites and pig gores, and counted out hundreds of white pills into hundreds of horny brown hands; while all space and light were effectively closed off by waiting patients and relatives."

Much of the excitement in the marshes came from hunting the wild boars that foraged through the reed beds. It was a highly dangerous exercise; Thesiger himself came close to being gored on several occasions and became adept at sewing up less fortunate marshmen who had been spiked on the tusks of the male boars or bitten by the sows. Thesiger shot some two thousand boars in the marshes with his .275 Rigby rifle, but admits he often wondered how long his luck would last. "Your nerve goes in the end."

Even in the depths of the marshes times were changing. By 1958 Thesiger found that transistors blaring tunes from Radio Baghdad were beginning to replace the traditional songs the marshmen had sung over the centuries as they cut reeds. And then in 1958, while Thesiger was in Europe, revolution swept through Baghdad; King Feisal was murdered, the British embassy was sacked. The door to the marshes was closed.

Since then he has never formed the same deep attachment for any new region, although his travels have never ceased. He has made a veritable odyssey of journeys to the mountains of the Hindu Kush, to the Atlas Mountains of Morocco, and to Yemen, and he once undertook a thousand-mile walk through Iran. He also returned to Ethiopia for two arduous expeditions down toward the Kenya border. He planned a third such trek in 1961 from Addis Ababa to the shores of Lake Rudolf in northern Kenya, but could not obtain the necessary permits. Instead he decided to approach Lake Rudolf from the south, walking up from Isiolo. He found to his delight that the deserts of northern Kenya around the lake were remote and unspoiled, the tribesmen living in the area still almost untouched by civilization. Throughout the 1960's he returned to Kenya again and again, and his journeys there add up to a remarkable achievement. He has walked as extensively in the deserts of northern Kenya as any white man today. Much of it is extremely hard going in temperatures of 140 degrees in the sun, 110 in the shade. Volcanic debris is widespread, so that progress is made only by a series of jumps from boulder to boulder. On one of these journeys, with a European companion, he pulled his Achilles' tendon. He refused, however, to abandon the expedition and kept walking for a month through this

In a primitive Venice of Iraq two marsh Arabs canoe past reed huts. From 1950 to 1958 Thesiger explored this desolate world of swamps and marshes between the Tigris and Euphrates.

rugged terrain while the tendon gradually healed.

This resolution not to fall short on any journey is one reason why Thesiger is normally most reluctant to take European companions with him. He fears they will not be able to keep up with his own grueling pace or live his Spartan life.

He has never felt any desire to plunge into new environments in the Far East or South America. "All my journeys have been linked," he points out. "There is a continuity through all the peoples of Morocco, the Sudan, Kenya, Arabia, Persia, and even northern Pakistan. Most of them are nomads, most are Moslems. If I went to South America, I would have to begin all over again—it would be quite outside my experience."

It is remarkable that a man of sixty can lead such a physically trying life. His frame is still as tough as the ash of a longbow. His mental outlook, which combines a complete fearlessness with a fatalism more akin to the Arab than to the European tradition, has undoubtedly carried him over hurdles that have felled men just as strong physically as he is.

As his reputation as an explorer has spread, he has found that on his short visits to Britain his mother's flat becomes a mecca for a new generation of restless young men in search of adventure. "All these young men come to

me asking where can we go? What can we do? I have to tell them there are very few places left which have not been penetrated by the machine."

Between conversations he walks through the Chelsea streets on his way back from lunch at the Traveller's Club, watching children play in the restricted space of a city park. It only confirms his view that man in an urban environment that is enslaved to technology is on a suicide course. He deplores the fact that we all appear sold on the virtues and benefits of our own Western civilization and are busy exporting it to everyone else. "Each society in the past has adapted to its environment so that the Turkhana or the Bedu or the Scottish crofter are all bound to be different from, say, the South Sea Islander. And each society has evolved its own set of rules, its own culture. Now we've decided to convince others that ours is right. Having had countries in Africa or the Middle East under our control, we've forced them to our pattern, our codes, our idea of civilization—a huge export drive of Western civilization regardless of whether it suits them or not. I'm quite convinced it doesn't."

This article is taken from Timothy S. Green's book Restless Spirit: Profiles of Adventure, *to be published by Walker & Co. later this year. Mr. Green is a former London correspondent for* HORIZON.

MY (UGH!) SENSITIVITY TRAINING

In his article on "The Flight from Reason" (page 4) Thomas Meehan writes of the flourishing new centers of "sensitivity training." For a firsthand report on one such center, here is the distinguished novelist Jean Stafford.

I was born in Southern California, but I was transplanted when I was six, and I have never been back. In a general way, though, I am aware of the frolicsome fads that originate there and spread overnight across the nation. But it is not possible to keep up with every fungus that springs from that rich mycelium, and until several months ago I had not heard about a new bee—to change my metaphor—in the collective bonnet, known as "sensitivity training." And then, unwittingly, I found myself a "trainee" in a "sensitivity training group," or to the fond cognoscenti, a "T group." I had been asked by a magazine to take part in, and write about, what I thought was "an experiment in anonymity," and I was given to understand that my fellows would be doctors, lawyers, merchants, and chiefs. We would all conceal from one another our occupations, our geographies, our family connections, and our aim would be to deduce these vital statistics from our conversation, our accents, our vocabularies, and, I supposed, our clothes and mannerisms. And so, under the impression that I was going to join a Sherlock Holmes party for a few days, I accepted the assignment with good humor, assuming that my playmates in the charade would be as carefree as I.

The moment I reached our rendezvous, my interest began to wane, and when I learned the rules of the game, it perished, not to be revived. We, who were twenty women in middle age divided up into two groups, were to remain within the walls of our meeting place from early Sunday evening until twelve noon the following Saturday, taking our meals together in a cafeteria and sleeping two to a room. The meals were to be our only diversion; for the rest of the time we were to sit about, looking at one another's shoes and hair, "relating." In our midst was a trainer—a woman who asked unanswerable questions like, "Jean, right this minute, how are you relating to Mildred?" Since I could not distinguish between Mildred and Inez and was, in any case, reciting the names of the states in alphabetical order to pass the time, she had me at a disadvantage. Small talk was out; by this I mean that we were to steer clear of any mention of politics, religion, science, books, the Vietnam war, civil rights, NASA, the AEC, the UN, LSD, Chicago, Mississippi, or castles in Spain. We were to purge ourselves of our histories, our memories, our opinions, and our sensibilities and "to jointly discover and interpret behavior as it occurs." We were to fling all inhibition to the winds and frankly speak our minds in order to be *honest* and *free*.

I lasted from Sunday until Tuesday, and then I left, revolted, bored silly. After a few days of total solitude during which I read a good deal of Jane Austen and Henry James and thought much upon such matters as decorum and the holding of the tongue, I unleashed *my* tongue and wrote an outraged letter to the prosperous businessman who had sponsored this game of dirty pool. Here is the broadside in full: "Dear Mr. Z.,

Miss X tells me you were distressed that I left before the end of the camp meeting.

Even if I had not been so profoundly offended by the squalid display of personal feeling insisted upon by your 'trainer,' a woman of stunning ineptitude and feloniously slovenly attire; even if I had not been so displeased by the unfastidious circumstance of sharing a bedroom with a strange woman of alarming avoirdupois and excruciatingly embarrassing coquettishness (it was a miracle she didn't propose a pillow fight); even if I had not been asked to lie on the floor with a sheet over my head on a hot day and told that I would experience 'a return to the womb,' an unlikely prophecy but nonetheless a most unseating one; or had not been enjoined to judge my companions in the three categories of 'the friendly helper,' 'the strong achiever,' or 'the logical thinker'; even if all these disgusting matters had not obtained, I would have left because of the perpetual and wanton abuse of the language.

Your trainer, *soi-disant,* and the trainees spoke almost wholly in the kind of cant that I do not choose to hear. They spoke of 'value words,' of 'job situations,' of 'life style,' of 'feeling level,' and, sometimes, of '*gut* feeling level.' They said 'simplistic' when they meant 'simple,' 'formalistic' when they meant 'formal'; they said 'home' when they meant 'house,' and 'area' when they meant 'room' or 'neighborhood.' They used 'structure' as a verb and 'construct' as a noun, and forever on their lips were such bastardisms as 'verbalize,' 'intellectualize,' 'externalize,' 'judgmental.' There seems to be an action, quite inscrutable, known as 'psyching out.' The mindless neologism 'confidentiality' was written in Palmer Method on the blackboard.

Apart from being assailed by bad taste, unspeakable logorrhea, and want of control, by a basic and irremediable stupidity and studious speciousness, I was bored very nearly to the point of paralysis. Among other things you told me before the crypto-evangelical sessions began, there was this whopping lie: you said the time would fly. I have never in my long life undergone such stultifying tedium.

You and your confederates are attempting to debase a once respectable discipline, that is, psychology, to the level of the shell game. Moreover, your ultimate goal can only be the destruction of what mankind has been about for the past five thousand years, that is, dignity and mercy and hope of excellence.

One trusts that the moral aristocracy will survive despite the venality and impurity of frivolous dabblers and manipulators who hold out the promise of 'more meaningful' lives through bad manners. Sensitivity training indeed! How is this most personal, most highly idiosyncratic, most *private* quality going to be acquired by squabbling in a *group*?

In the most sincere disapprobation,
Jean Stafford"
"P.S. A suggestion: hereafter select trainers who look a little less like Ma and Pa Kettle."

By JEAN STAFFORD